THE TERRY LECTURES

# Reason, Faith and Revolution

OTHER TERRY EAGLETON TITLES
FROM SEAGULL BOOKS

*The Function of Criticism*

*On Evil*

*Why Marx was Right*

TERRY EAGLETON

# Reason, Faith and Revolution

## Reflections on the God Debate

Seagull Books

CALCUTTA 2012

First published by Yale University Press, 2009



Reprinted by arrangement with Yale University Press

For sale only in South Asia
(India, Pakistan, Nepal, Bhutan, Bangladesh, Sri Lanka and the Maldives)

Jacket designed by Sunandini Banerjee, Seagull Books

Seagull Books, 2012

ISBN 978 8 17046 347 4

*Published by Naveen Kishore on behalf of Seagull Books Private Limited*
*31A, S. P. Mukherjee Road, Calcutta 700 025*

*Typeset in Adobe type by Keystone Typesetting, Inc., USA*
*Printed and bound by Hyam Enterprises, Calcutta, India*

*In memory of Leo Pyle*

*The Dwight Harrington Terry Foundation Lectures on Religion in the Light of Science and Philosophy*

The deed of gift declares that "the object of this foundation is not the promotion of scientific investigation and discovery, but rather the assimilation and interpretation of that which has been or shall be hereafter discovered, and its application to human welfare, especially by the building of the truths of science and philosophy into the structure of a broadened and purified religion. The founder believes that such a religion will greatly stimulate intelligent effort for the improvement of human conditions and the advancement of the race in strength and excellence of character. To this end it is desired that a series of lectures be given by men eminent in their respective departments, on ethics, the history of civilization and religion, biblical research, all sciences and branches of knowledge which have an important bearing on the subject, all the great laws of nature, especially of evolution . . . also such interpretations of literature and sociology as are in accord with the spirit of this foundation, to the end that the

Christian spirit may be nurtured in the fullest light of the world's knowledge and that mankind may be helped to attain its highest possible welfare and happiness upon this earth." The present work constitutes the latest volume published on this foundation.

# Contents

# Preface

Religion has wrought untold misery in human affairs. For the most part, it has been a squalid tale of bigotry, superstition, wishful thinking, and oppressive ideology. I therefore have a good deal of sympathy with its rationalist and humanist critics. But it is also the case, as this book argues, that most such critics buy their rejection of religion on the cheap. When it comes to the New Testament, at least, what they usually write off is a worthless caricature of the real thing, rooted in a degree of ignorance and prejudice to match religion's own. It is as though one were to dismiss feminism on the basis of Clint Eastwood's opinions of it.

It is with this ignorance and prejudice that I take issue in this book. If the agnostic left cannot afford such intellectual indolence when it comes to the Jewish and Christian Scriptures, it is not only because it belongs to justice and honesty to confront your opponent at his or her most convincing. It is also that radicals might discover there some valuable insights into human emancipation, in an era where the political left stands in dire need of good ideas. I do not invite such readers to believe in these ideas, any more than I myself believe in the archangel Gabriel, the infallibility of the pope, the idea that Jesus walked on water, or the claim that he rose up into heaven before the eyes of his disciples. If I try in this book to "ventriloquize" what I take to be a version of the Christian gospel relevant to radicals and humanists, I do not wish to be mistaken for a dummy. But the Jewish and Christian scriptures have much to say about some vital questions—death, suffering, love, self-dispossession, and the like—on which the left has for the most part maintained an embarrassed silence. It is time for this politically crippling shyness to come to an end.

This book is based on the Dwight H. Terry Lectures which I delivered at Yale University in April 2008. I have preserved the conversational tone of a lecture to begin with, but this rapidly fades into a more conventional style of argument. I am deeply grateful to the Trustees of the Terry Lectures, and in particular to Laurelee Field, for making my stay in New Haven so socially agreeable and intellectually rewarding. The same goes for the many students and academics who attended the sessions.

Reason, Faith, & Revolution

CHAPTER ONE

# The Scum of the Earth

It was, I felt, characteristic of the delightfully informal nature of American society that I should receive a letter from Yale inviting me to deliver the Terry Lectures. I had of course long been accustomed to the instant-first-name character of U.S. culture, but this long-range intimacy nevertheless came as something of a surprise. I began to wonder whether these talks, when Carl Jung was delivering them, were affectionately known as the Chuck Lectures, to be changed later to the Maggie Lectures when the speaker was Margaret Mead. Anyway, I feel that something is demanded of me in return for this spontaneous display of geniality; so I insist that while I am here at Yale I should be known not as Professor Eagleton, but as Doctor Eagleton. Let no one claim that we Brits don't know how to unbend.

My delight at this informality was quickly tempered as I read on to discover that the Terry Lectures are traditionally devoted to two subjects I know embarrassingly little about, namely science and religion. As for the relationship between them, which is of particular concern to the Terry Lectures, one of my few experiences of this came in my childhood in the form of a monstrous, universally feared and detested head-master called Brother Columba, a chemist and cleric whose religion was as brutally impersonal as the laws of science, and who as an authoritarian Roman Catholic was a good deal more at home with test tubes than with human beings.[1]

I have, however, never allowed ignorance to deter me from anything, which is why I stand before you today—though I must confess that I did begin my intellectual career as an amateur species of theologian, in those heady post–Second Vatican Council days in the 1960s in which anyone able to spell the name Schillebeeckx was instantly drafted onto the editorial board of some opaque theological journal based in Nijmegen. All I can claim in this respect is that I think I may know just about enough theology to be able to spot when someone like Richard Dawkins or Christopher Hitchens, a couple I shall henceforth reduce for convenience to the single signifier "Ditchkins," is talking out of the back of his neck. Before I conflate Hitchens and Dawkins too peremptorily, however, let me draw a contrast between the stylish, entertaining, splendidly impassioned, compulsively readable quality of the former's *God Is Not Great* and Dawkins's *The God Delusion,* which merits absolutely none of these epithets. Dawkins's doctrinal ferocity has begun to eat into his prose style. Perhaps I should add that when Christopher Hitchens was still a humble Chris, he and I were comrades in the same far-left political outfit. But he has gone on to higher things, discovering in the process a degree of political maturity as a naturalized citizen of Babylon, whereas I have remained stuck in the same old political groove, a case of arrested development if ever there was one.

I should also confess that since the only theology I don't know much about is Christian theology, as opposed to those kinds I know nothing at all about, I shall confine my discussion to that alone, on the grounds that it is better to be provincial than presumptuous. As for science, my knowledge of it is largely confined to the fact that it is greeted with dark suspicion by most postmodernists—a sound enough reason in my view for enthusiastically endorsing almost anything it cares to say. As well as science and religion, I shall also be speaking in these lectures about politics, which means that two of my three subjects, politics and religion, happen to be the two traditionally banned from discussion in English pubs.

Much as I dislike the practice of autobiography,[2] a personal word is scarcely avoidable here. I was brought up as a conventional Roman Catholic of Irish provenance in working-class England, and imbibed in my childhood a set of baroque and hermetic doctrines which, so I was astonished to discover later, were supposed to have some sort of bearing on human existence. It was rather like being raised in a strictly observant Marxist family, learning at one's parents' knee a number of formulas about the negation of the negation and the transformation of quantity into quality, without a clue that all this was supposed to have some sort of relevance to questions of human freedom and justice. Since the religious doctrine I was taught seemed to me as I approached student age to illuminate human existence about as profoundly as the croakings of a frog, it seemed natural when I arrived at university to discard this whole way of talking in the name of something rather more relevant and humane.

In the Cambridge of the early 1960s, this was known among other things as existentialism, a term which was for the most part an ontologically imposing way of saying that one was nineteen, far from home, feeling rather blue, and like a toddler in a play school hadn't much of a clue as to what was going on. A few decades later this condition persisted among late adolescents, but it was now known as post-structuralism. But there was also socialism, which I had encountered while growing up along with Irish Republicanism, and which—in an era of Cold War hostilities, weapons of mass destruction, and anticolonial revolution—seemed a touch more relevant to the human species than the doctrine of limbo (a spiritual condition not to be confused with a popular Caribbean dance), or recalling the

Latin name for the precise type of worship appropriate to those drearily bureaucratic subcommittees known as the saints.

Things, however, didn't prove quite so simple. For no sooner had I arrived in Cambridge, at a point where any reasonably sensitive, moderately perceptive character would have rejected for the nonsense it largely was what I had learned at school, than the Second Vatican Council broke out, along with a version of the Christian gospel which seemed to me to make some rather urgent human and political sense. This, needless to say, brought its frustrations. The rethinking it entailed looked like involving a lot of tedious spade work, as the character in P. G. Wodehouse remarked when his interlocutor seemed not to understand the word "pig." For it is of course always easier to buy one's rejection of a belief system on the cheap, by (for example) triumphantly dismissing out of hand a version of Christianity that only seriously weird types, some of them lurking sheepishly in caves too ashamed to come out and confront the rest of us, would espouse in the first place. This applies to more than religion. It is easier to believe that Nietzsche was a budding Nazi than to grasp that he was a precursor of Foucault. To save yourself too laborious an attention to Marxism, you can dismiss it on the grounds that it dreams of a world of equality in which men and women will all be spiritually wretched and materially miserable in exactly the same way.

The so-called new theology I stumbled upon at the age of eighteen or so, with the aid of a few maverick Dominicans and rather more pints of bitter, was not in fact new at all. It was new only to the likes of callow young papists like myself. It did not see God the Creator as some kind of mega-manufacturer or cosmic chief executive officer, as the Richard Dawkins school of nineteenth-century liberal rationalism tends to imagine—what the theologian Herbert McCabe calls "the idolatrous notion of God as a very large and powerful creature."[3] Dawkins falsely considers that Christianity offers a rival view of the universe to science. Like the philosopher Daniel C. Dennett in *Breaking the Spell,* he thinks it is a kind of bogus theory or pseudo-explanation of the world. In this sense, he is rather like someone who thinks that a novel is a botched piece of sociology, and who therefore can't see the point of it at all. Why bother with Robert Musil when you can read Max Weber?

For Thomas Aquinas, by contrast, God the Creator is not a hypothesis about how the world originated. It does not compete, say, with the theory that the universe resulted from a random fluctuation in a quantum vacuum. In fact, Aquinas was quite ready to entertain the possibility that the world had no origin at all. Dawkins makes an error of genre, or category mistake, about the kind of thing Christian belief is. He imagines that it is either some kind of pseudo-science, or that, if it is not that, then it conveniently dispenses itself from the need for evidence altogether. He also has an old-fashioned scientistic notion of what constitutes evidence. Life for Dawkins would seem to divide neatly down the middle between things you can prove beyond all doubt, and blind faith. He fails to see that all the most interesting stuff goes on in neither of these places. Christopher Hitchens makes much the same crass error, claiming in *God Is Not Great* that "thanks to the telescope and the microscope, [religion] no longer offers an explanation of anything important."[4] But Christianity was never meant to be an *explanation* of anything in the first place. It is rather like saying that thanks to the electric toaster we can forget about Chekhov.

The New Testament has next to nothing to say about God as Creator. Indeed, I suppose that where science and religion come closest for the Christian is not in what they say about the world, but in the act of creative imagination which both projects involve—a creative act which the believer finds the source of in the Holy Spirit. Scientists like Heisenberg or Schrödinger are supreme imaginative artists, who when it comes to the universe are aware that the elegant and beautiful are more likely to be true than the ugly and misshapen. From a scientific standpoint, cosmic truth is in the deepest sense a question of style, as Plato, the Earl of Shaftesbury, and John Keats were aware. And this is at least one sense in which science is thoroughly and properly value-laden.

God for Christian theology is not a mega-manufacturer. He is rather what sustains all things in being by his love, and would still be this even if the world had no beginning. Creation is not about getting things off the ground. Rather, God is the reason why there is something rather than nothing, the condition of possibility of any entity whatsoever. Not being any sort of entity himself, however, he is not to be reckoned up alongside these things, any more than my envy and my left foot constitute a pair of objects. God and the universe do not make two. In an act of Judaic iconoclasm, we are forbidden to make graven images of this nonentity because the only image of him is human beings. There is a document that records God's endless, dispiriting struggle with organized religion, known as the Bible. God the Creator is not a celestial engineer at work on a superbly rational design that will impress his research grant body no end, but an artist, and an aesthete to boot, who made the world with no functional end in view but simply for the love and delight of it.

Or, as one might say in more theological language, for the hell of it. He made it as gift, superfluity, and gratuitous gesture—out of nothing, rather than out of grim necessity. In fact, for Christian theology there is no necessity to the world at all, and God may have long ago bitterly regretted succumbing to the sentimental impulse which inspired him to throw it off in the first place. He created it out of love, not need. There was nothing in it for him. The Creation is the original *acte gratuit.* The doctrine that the world was made out of nothing is meant to alert us to the mind-blowing contingency of the cosmos—the fact that like a modernist work of art it might just as well never have happened, and like most thoughtful men and women is perpetually overshadowed by the possibility of its own nonexistence. Creation "out of nothing" is not testimony to how devilishly clever God is, dispensing as he can with even the most rudimentary raw materials, but to the fact that the world is not the inevitable culmination of some prior process, the upshot of some inexorable chain of cause and effect. Any such preceding chain of causality would have to be part of the world, and so could not count as the origin of it. Because there is no necessity about the cosmos, we cannot deduce the laws which govern it from a priori principles, but need instead to look at how it actually works. This is the task of science. There is thus a curious connection between the doctrine of creation out of nothing and the professional life of Richard Dawkins. Without God, Dawkins would be out of a job. It is thus particularly churlish of him to call the existence of his employer into question.

The existence of the world, then, is a critique of iron causality, and thus testimony to the freedom of which Ditchkins, in personal and political terms, is so rightly jealous. The world thus belongs to that exceedingly rare class of objects which, in a way that would have delighted the heart of Oscar Wilde, exist entirely for their own sake and for no drearily utilitarian end—a category which along with God includes art, evil, and humanity. It is part of the world's sharing in God's own freedom that it works all by itself. Unlike George Bush, God is not an interventionist kind of ruler. It is this autonomy of the world which makes science and Richard Dawkins possible in the first place. Ditchkins, who holds that there is no need to bring God into scientific investigation, might be interested to learn that the greatest theologian in history, the Aquinas to whom I have just alluded, thoroughly agreed. Science is properly atheistic. Science and theology are for the most part not talking about the same kind of things, any more than orthodontics and literary criticism are. This is one reason for the grotesque misunderstandings that arise between them.

God, in short, is every bit as gloriously pointless as Ditchkins tells us he is. He is a kind of perpetual critique of instrumental reason. John C. Lennox writes in *God's Undertaker* that some scientists and philosophers think we should not ask after the reason for the universe because, according to them, there isn't one.[5] In this, however, they are unwittingly at one with theologians. If we are God's creatures, it is in the first place because, like him, we exist (or should exist) purely for the pleasure of it. The question raised by radical Romanticism, which for these purposes includes Karl Marx, is that of what political transformations would be necessary for this to become possible in practice. Jesus, unlike most responsible American citizens, appears to do no work, and is accused of being a glutton and a drunkard. He is presented as homeless, propertyless, celibate, peripatetic, socially marginal, disdainful of kinsfolk, without a trade, a friend of outcasts and pariahs, averse to material possessions, without fear for his own safety, careless about purity regulations, critical of traditional authority, a thorn in the side of the Establishment, and a scourge of the rich and powerful. Though he was no revolutionary in the modern sense of the term, he has something of the lifestyle of one. He sounds like a cross between a hippie and a guerilla fighter. He respects the Sabbath not because it means going to church but because it represents a temporary escape from the burden of labor. The Sabbath is about resting, not religion. One of the best reasons for being a Christian, as for being a socialist, is that you don't like having to work, and reject the fearful idolatry of it so rife in countries like the United States. Truly civilized societies do not hold predawn power breakfasts.

The quarrel between science and theology, then, is not a matter of how the universe came about, or which approach can provide the best "explanation" for it. It is a disagreement about how far back one has to go, though not in the chronological sense. For theology, science does not start far back enough—not in the sense that it fails to posit a Creator, but in the sense that it does not ask questions such as why there is anything in the first place, or why what we do have is actually intelligible to us. Perhaps these are phony questions anyway; some philosophers certainly think so. But theologians, as Rowan Williams has argued, are interested in the question of why we ask for explanations at all, or why we assume that the universe hangs together in a way that makes explanation possible.[6] Where do our notions of explanation, regularity, and intelligibility come from? How do we explain rationality and intelligibility themselves, or is this question either superfluous or too hard to answer? Can we not account for rationality because to do so is to presuppose it? Whatever we think of such queries, science as we know it is possible only because the world displays a certain internal order and coherence—

possible, that is to say, for roughly aesthetic reasons. Is it relevant to inquire where these laws come from? Might science one day find out, or is this question off-bounds to it?

Is it a matter for wonderment that we can understand so much of the deep structure of the universe, to no apparent evolutionary advantage? Or is it just a fortunate contingency? Was Einstein onto something or simply waxing poetic when he observed that "the most incomprehensible thing about the universe is that it is comprehensible,"[7] adding as he did that one would not a priori expect such a high degree of order in the world? There are those for whom the spectacular successes of science have rendered religion redundant; and there are others for whom those successes spring from a fundamental fact—that our minds seem somehow attuned to the fundamental stuff of the world—which is itself cause for metaphysical reflection.

Why is it that mathematics, of all things, seems to encode the intelligibility of the physical universe, and is it reasonable for science to take this, along with the uniformity of physical laws, simply as an article of faith? Is it equally reasonable for science to place its faith in the consistency of mathematics, even when Gödel's second theorem demonstrates that it cannot be proved? Do we too easily take for granted the fact that before we have even come to reason, the world is open and available to us in the first place? Instead of just asking for reasons or explanations, should not science be struck by all the complex stage-setting which this demands?

Even if these meta-questions are valid, which one may well take leave to doubt, they do not necessarily evoke the answer "because of God." The philosopher Martin Heidegger, whose thought some in Anglo-Saxon circles consider so deep as to be meaningless, raised questions of this kind, but was certainly no religious believer. You do not need to go to church to ponder issues like this. But the point is that you do not need to be a scientist either. There is no more need for scientists to raise these questions than there is for trapeze artists to do so. This is one sense in which theology (or metaphysics) and science are different sorts of pursuit.

To see God as completely pointless, and the moral life as much the same, is not to deny that instrumental reason has its place. There would, for example, be no emancipatory politics without it, and no science or technology either. Aestheticians are seized by the beauty and sensuous particularity of things, theologians by the fact that their existence is so mind-bendingly contingent; while scientists and technologists have to press these things into the knowledge and service of humankind, and so cannot afford to spend all their time emitting grunts of pleasure or shouts of astonishment. Even so, on this theological view, morality is quite as pointless as the universe itself. It is a question of how to live most richly and enjoyably, relishing one's powers and capacities purely for their own sake. This self-delighting energy, which is entirely without point or function, stands in no need of justification before some grim-faced tribunal of History, Duty, *Geist,* Production, Utility, or Teleology. One can contrast this view of ethics with the Kantian case that if what you do feels pleasant, it is unlikely to be virtuous. (I am simplifying *The Critique of Practical Reason* a little here, as you may have noticed.) The morality Jesus preaches is reckless, extravagant, improvident, over-the-top, a scandal to actuaries and a stumbling block to real estate agents: forgive your enemies, give away your cloak as well as your coat, turn the other cheek, love those who insult you, walk the extra mile, take no thought for tomorrow.

Christopher Hitchens greets this creative recklessness with petit bourgeois distaste: "The analogy of humans to lilies," he bristles like an indignant bank manager, ". . . suggests—along with many other injunctions—that things like thrift, innovation, family life, and so forth are a sheer waste of time" (118). There is indeed good evidence, one is gratified to report, that the New Testament considers the family largely a waste of time. We shall be looking at this a bit later. Hitchens is also unable to see much point in the scriptural injunction to conceal from your left hand what your right hand is doing, which is of course a warning against trumpeting your good deeds to the world. Since a vein of consistent self-vaunting runs through the writings of the later Hitchens, this particular blind spot is scarcely surprising. Neither he nor Dawkins is afflicted with an excess of modesty. He also dismisses the so-called beatitudes as "fanciful wish-thinking about the meek and the peacemakers" (117). In fact, one wonders why his friends in the Pentagon haven't sought to ban this insidious propaganda for peace and the poor altogether. Jesus fails miserably to talk like a five-star general.

Jesus probably preached this kind of ethic because he thought the end of the world was just round the corner, which turns out to have been rather a grave miscalculation. His sense of history seems to have been a little awry. In fact, he would no doubt have had no sense of secular history at all in our own sense of the term. Even so, it is not the kind of morality one associates with chartered accountants or oil executives. Because God is transcendent—that's to say, because he doesn't need humanity, having fashioned us just for the fun of it—he is not neurotically possessive of us. He needs us no more than one needs a pet mongoose or a tattoo. He is therefore able to let us be; and the word for this is freedom, which is where for Christian theology we belong to him most deeply.

There is a sense in which replacing a transcendent God with an omnipotent humanity alters surprisingly little, as Nietzsche scornfully pointed out. There is still a stable metaphysical center to the world; it is just that it is now us, rather than a deity. And since we are sovereign, bound by no constraints which we do not legislate for ourselves, we can exercise our newfound divinity by indulging among other things in that form of ecstatically creative *jouissance* known as destruction. In Nietzsche's view, the death of God must also spell the death of Man—that is to say, the end of a certain lordly, overweening humanism—if absolute power is not simply to be transplanted from the one to the other. Otherwise humanism will always be secretly theological. It will be a continuation of God by other means. God will simply live a shadowy afterlife in the form of respectable suburban morality, as indeed he does today. The infinity of Man would simply end up doing service for the eternity of God. In Faustian spirit, Man would fall in love with his own apparently boundless powers, forgetful that God in the doctrine of the Incarnation is shown to be in love with the fleshly, frail, and finite. Besotted by his own infinity, Man would find himself in perpetual danger of developing too fast, overreaching himself and bringing himself to nothing, as in the myth of the Fall.

There is a traditional cure for this malady, one known as tragic art; but like chemotherapy the remedy can be almost as devastating as the sickness. When the ancient Greeks witnessed such unrestrained striving, they trembled and looked fearfully to the sky, aware that it would have its comeuppance. Saint Augustine observes that created things should not presume to create—not as a rebuke to artists, but to what we might now call the great bourgeois myth of self-origination. Self-authorship is the bourgeois fantasy par excellence. Denying that our freedom thrives only within the context of a more fundamental dependency lies at the root of a good deal of historical disaster. It is certainly one of the driving forces of Western neo-imperialism today.

For orthodox Christian doctrine, it is our dependence on God that allows us to be self-determining, as it is our dependence on language or history or culture which allows us to come into our own as persons. God for Thomas Aquinas is the power that allows us to be ourselves, rather as the love of our parents allows us to be ourselves. We can fantasize like Oedipal children that we would be more free by breaking loose from the sources of our life, but this is self-deception. Instead, our parents have to find a way of nourishing us which also contains the potential to let us go, so that their love can become the ground of our independence rather than the impediment to it. D. H. Lawrence's great novel *The Rainbow* ponders this paradox, in charting the various generations of a family.

This, then, is what it means to say that God has created us in his own image and likeness, since he himself is pure liberty. It follows that he is also the ground of our ability to reject him—which is to say that in a splendidly big-hearted gesture, he is the source of atheism as well as faith. He is not a censorious power which prevents us from being good middle-class liberals and thinking for ourselves. This is simply the primitive, Philip Pullman–like view of those who cannot wean themselves off the idea of God as Big Daddy. The poet William Blake would have had nothing but scorn for this naïve misconception. What writers like Pullman do not see is that the liberal doctrine of freedom derives among other sources from the Christian notion of free will, rather as the liberal belief in progress has a distant resonance of Christian ideas of Providence. As John Gray writes, "The key liberal theorists of toleration are John Locke, who defended religious freedom in explicitly Christian terms, and Benedict Spinoza, a Jewish rationalist who was also a mystic."[8]

To highlight such affinities between liberalism and Judeo-Christianity (and there are many more) is in no sense to disparage the great liberal or Enlightenment heritage.[9] Some Marxists are churlishly reluctant to acknowledge that Marx owes a good deal to the Judaic tradition; but why should they have such a low opinion of that lineage as to regard this claim as somehow devaluing his work? Liberalism (or radicalism) and religious faith are not necessarily at odds with each other, whatever Ditchkins might think. Many Muslim thinkers have claimed a compatibility between Islam and socialism. A good deal of nineteenth-century Protestant theology is profoundly shaped by the liberal legacy. Friedrich Nietzsche did not oppose liberalism to Christianity in the manner of Ditchkins. He saw them as pretty much of a piece and condemned them both, as the Nazis and the Stalinists were to do later. D. H. Lawrence does much the same in *Women in Love.* Secular liberalism is in no sense the "natural" antidote to religious faith.

The non-God or anti-God of Scripture, who hates burnt offerings and acts of smug self-righteousness, is the enemy of idols, fetishes, and graven images of all kinds—gods, churches, ritual sacrifice, the Stars and Stripes, nations, sex, success, ideologies, and the like. You shall know him for who he is when you see the hungry being filled with good things and the rich being sent empty away. Salvation, rather bathetically, turns out to be not a matter of cult, law, and ritual, of special observances and conformity to a moral code, of slaughtering animals for sacrifice or even of being splendidly virtuous. It is a question of feeding the hungry, welcoming the immigrants, visiting the sick, and protecting the poor, orphaned and widowed from the violence of the rich. Astonishingly, we are saved not by a special apparatus known as religion, but by the quality of our everyday relations with one another. It was Christianity, not the French intelligentsia, which invented the concept of everyday life.[10]

There is nothing heroic about the New Testament at all. Jesus is a sick joke of a savior. Messiahs are not born in stables. They are high-born, heroic warriors who will lead the nation in battle against its enemies. They do not reject weapons of destruction, enter the national capital riding on donkeys, or get themselves strung up. From the viewpoint of Jewish tradition, a murdered Messiah is as much an outrageous anomaly or contradiction in terms as the sentence "Ditchkins then humbly allowed that there was something to be said for the other side." Christianity is all rather disappointingly materialist, unglamorous, and prosaic. "Render unto Caesar the things that are Caesar's, and to God the things that are God's" is a notoriously enigmatic injunction; but whatever it means, it is unlikely to mean that religion is one thing whereas politics is another, a peculiarly modern prejudice if ever there was one. Any devout Jew of Jesus's time would have known that the things that are God's include working for justice, welcoming the immigrants, and humbling the high-and-mighty. The whole cumbersome paraphernalia of religion is to be replaced by another kind of temple, that of the murdered, transfigured body of Jesus. To the outrage of the Zealots, Pharisees, and right-wing rednecks of all ages, this body is dedicated in particular to all those losers, deadbeats, riffraff, and colonial collaborators who are not righteous but flamboyantly unrighteous—who either live in chronic transgression of the Mosaic law or, like the Gentiles, fall outside its sway altogether.

These men and women are not being asked to bargain their way into God's favor by sacrificing beasts, fussing about their diet, or being impeccably well-behaved. Instead, the good news is that God loves them anyway, in all their moral squalor. Jesus's message is that God is on their side despite their viciousness—that the source of inexhaustibly self-delighting life he calls his Father is neither judge, patriarch, accuser, nor superego, but lover, friend, fellow-accused, and counsel for the defense. The biblical name for God as judge or accuser is Satan, which literally means "adversary." Satan is a way of seeing God as a great big bully, which as we shall see in a moment is a peculiarly rewarding image of him. Men and women are called upon to do nothing apart from acknowledge the fact that God is on their side no matter what, in the act of loving assent which is known as faith. In fact, Jesus has very little to say about sin at all, unlike a great many of his censorious followers. His mission is to accept men and women's frailty, not to rub their noses in it.

It is this overturning of the Satanic or super-egoic image of God in Jesus that offers to unlock the lethal deadlock between Law and desire, or what Jacques Lacan calls the Real. It is a condition in which we come to fall morbidly in love with the Law itself, and with the oppressed, unhappy state to which it reduces us, desiring nothing more than to punish ourselves for our guilt even unto death. This is why Saint Paul describes the Law as cursed. It is this urge to do away with ourselves as so much waste and garbage to which Freud gives the name of the death drive, the opposite of which is an unconditionally accepting love. As Paul writes, the Law, and the sin or guilt which it generates, is what brings death into the world. The choice is one between a life liberated from this pathological deadlock, which is known to the Gospel as eternal life, and that grisly caricature of eternal life which is the ghastly pseudo-immortality of the death drive. It is a state in which we prevent ourselves from dying for real by clinging desperately to our morbid pleasure in death as a way of affirming that we are alive. It is this spectral, dead-but-won't-lie-down state of existence, that of Pinkie in Graham Greene's novel *Brighton Rock* or Pincher Martin in William Golding's novel of that title, which represents the living death known as hell.[11]

This is the hell not of traitors and toasting forks, but of those who are stuck fast in their masochistic delight in the Law, and spit in the face of those who offer to relieve them of this torture. If the God of the so-called Old Testament is portrayed from time to time as a sadistic ogre, one reason is that men and women can desire as well as fear the wrath of the superego. They can cling to their own oppression like a lover, and can go to almost any lengths not to relinquish the self-lacerating pleasure this yields them. To be unburdened of their guilt is to be deprived of the very sickness which keeps them going. This, one might claim, is the primary masochism known as religion. In this context, the good news that we are loved simply for what we are is bound to come as an intolerable affront. It threatens to rob us of the misery which at least proves that we still exist. It also seems to render pointless our laborious efforts at moral self-improvement. We do not want such a light yoke. Instead, we want to hug our chains.

For Christian teaching, God's love and forgiveness are ruthlessly unforgiving powers which break violently into our protective, self-rationalizing little sphere, smashing our sentimental illusions and turning our world brutally upside down. In Jesus, the law is revealed to be the law of love and mercy, and God not some Blakean Nobodaddy but a helpless, vulnerable animal. It is the flayed and bloody scapegoat of Calvary that is now the true signifier of the Law. Which is to say that those who are faithful to God's law of justice and compassion will be done away with by the state. If you don't love, you're dead, and if you do, they'll kill you. Here, then, is your pie in the sky or opium of the people, your soft-eyed consolation and pale-cheeked piety. Here is the fantasy and escapism that the hard-headed secularist pragmatist finds so distasteful. Freud saw religion as a mitigation of the harshness of the human condition; but it would surely be at least as plausible to claim that what we call reality is a mitigation of the Gospel's ruthless demands, which include such agreeable acts of escapism as being ready to lay down your life for a total stranger. Imitating Jesus means imitating his death as well as his life, since the two are not finally distinguishable. The death is the consummation of the life, the place where the ultimate meaning of Jesus's self-giving is revealed.

The only authentic image of this violently loving God is a tortured and executed political criminal, who dies in an act of solidarity with what the Bible calls the *anawim,* meaning the destitute and dispossessed. Crucifixion was reserved by the Romans for political offenses alone. The *anawim,* in Pauline phrase, are the shit of the earth—the scum and refuse of society who constitute the cornerstone of the new form of human life known as the kingdom of God. Jesus himself is consistently presented as their representative. His death and descent into hell is a voyage into madness, terror, absurdity, and self-dispossession, since only a revolution that cuts that deep can answer to our dismal condition.

What is at stake here is not a prudently reformist project of pouring new wine into old bottles, but an avant-gardist epiphany of the absolutely new—of a regime so revolutionary as to surpass all image and utterance, a reign of justice and fellowship which for the Gospel writers is even now striking into this bankrupt, *dépassé,* washed-up world. No middle ground is permitted here: the choice between justice and the powers of this world is stark and absolute, a matter of fundamental conflict and antithesis. What is at issue is a slashing sword, not peace, consensus, and negotiation. Jesus does not seem to be any sort of liberal, which is no doubt one grudge Ditchkins holds against him. He would not make a good committee man. Neither would he go down well on Wall Street, just as he did not go down well among the money changers of the Jerusalem temple.

Given the lamentable state of humanity, this unashamed utopia does not come easily. I mean by "lamentable state" the prevalence of greed, idolatry, and delusion, the depth of our instinct to dominate and possess, the dull persistence of injustice and exploitation, the chronic anxiety which leads us to hate, maim, and exploit, along with the sickness, suffering, and despair which Jesus associates with evil. All this is what Christianity knows as original sin. The coming of the kingdom involves not a change of government, but a turbulent passage through death, nothingness, madness, loss, and futility. It is this passage which in Christian mythology is signified among other things by Christ's descent into hell after his death. There is no possibility of a smooth evolution here. Given the twisted state of the world, self-fulfillment can ultimately come about only through self-divestment.

That this is so is a tragedy in itself. It would be far more agreeable if we could achieve justice and fellowship spontaneously, without having to die, personally and politically, to our selfishness, violence, possessiveness and urge to dominate. But at least this death is in the name of a more abundant life, not some masochistic self-violence. For the Gospel, there are two kinds of life-in-death—the living death which is hell, and the abundance of life which comes from being able to surrender one's self-possessiveness. They are not always easy to tell apart.

If self-denial is not an end in itself for Christianity, neither is celibacy. Jesus was probably celibate because he believed that the kingdom of God was about to arrive any moment, which left no time for mortgages, car washes, children, and other such distracting domestic phenomena. This brand of celibacy, however, is not hostile to sexuality as such. On the contrary, it sees giving up sex as a sacrifice, and sacrifice means abandoning something you hold precious. It is no sacrifice to give up drinking bleach. When Saint Paul looks for a sign (or "sacrament") of the future redeemed world, he offers us the sexual coupling of bodies. It is marriage, not celibacy, which is a sacrament. Fullness of life is what matters; but working for a more abundant life all round sometimes involves suspending or surrendering some of the good things that characterize that existence. Celibacy in this sense is a revolutionary option. Those who fight corrupt regimes in the jungles of Latin America want to go home, enjoy their children, and resume a normal life. The problem is that if this kind of existence is to be available to everyone, the guerilla fighter has to forgo such fulfillments for the moment. He or she thus becomes what the New Testament calls "a eunuch for the kingdom." The worst mistake would be to find in this enforced austerity an image of the good life as such. Revolutionaries are rarely the best image of the society they are working to create.

The most radical form of self-denial is to give up not cigarettes or whiskey but one's own body, an act which is traditionally known as martyrdom. The martyr yields up his or her most precious possession, but would prefer not to; the suicide, by contrast, is glad to be rid of a life that has become an unbearable burden. If Jesus wanted to die, then he was just another suicide, and his death was as worthless and futile as a suicide bomber's messy finale. Martyrs, as opposed to suicides, are those who place their deaths at the service of others. Even their dying is an act of love. Their deaths are such that they can bear fruit in the lives of others. This is true not only of those who die so that others may live (taking someone's place in the queue for the Nazi gas chambers, for example), but also of those who die in the defense of a principle which is potentially life-giving for others. The word "martyr" means "witness"; and what he or she bears witness to is a principle without which it may not be worth living in the first place. In this sense, the martyr's death testifies to the value of life, not to its unimportance. This is not the case with Islamic suicide bombers.

The transfigured existence that Jesus proclaims involves the passage of the reviled, polluted thing from weakness to power, death to life, agony to glory, for which the ancient name is not so much tragedy as sacrifice. In this way, the stumbling block can become the cornerstone, as the new order is constructed out of the scraps and leavings of the old. Only by a readiness to abandon our dished-up world can we live in the hope of a more authentic existence in the future. This doctrine is known not as pessimism but as realism. Because we cannot know for sure that such an existence is possible, in the sense that we can know the speed of light or the price of onions, this self-dispossession requires faith. We need to have faith that, against all appearances to the contrary, the powerless can come to power. Only by preserving a steadfast fidelity to failure, one scandalous to nations that despise a loser, can any human power prove fertile and durable. It is by virtue of this impossible, stonily disenchanted realism, staring the Medusa's head of the monstrous, traumatic, obscene Real of human crucifixion full in the face, that some kind of resurrection may be possible. Only by accepting this as the very last word, seeing everything else as so much sentimentalist garbage, ideological illusion, fake utopia, false consolation, ludicrously upbeat idealism—only then might it prove not to be quite the last word after all.

The New Testament is a brutal destroyer of human illusions. If you follow Jesus and don't end up dead, it appears you have some explaining to do. The stark signifier of the human condition is one who spoke up for love and justice and was done to death for his pains. The traumatic truth of human history is a mutilated body. Those who do not see this dreadful image of a tortured innocent as the truth of history are likely to adopt some bright-eyed superstition such as the dream of untrammeled human progress, for which, as we shall see, Ditchkins is a full-blooded apologist. There are rationalist myths as well as religious ones. Indeed, many secular myths are degutted versions of sacred ones.

Far from fostering some ghoulish cult of suffering, Jesus seems to regard physical sickness as unequivocally a form of evil, and opposes to it what he calls abundance of life—which is to say what the Gospel calls "eternal" life, life at its most richly and exuberantly human, intoxicated with its own high spirits and self-delight. For Christian faith, so I take it, the phrase "atheistic humanism" is not so much erroneous as oxymoronic, since there can be no full humanity without God. "Let the dead bury their own dead," Jesus brusquely informs his followers—a sentiment that the Jews of the time, for whom burial of the dead was a sacred duty and unburied corpses an unthinkable scandal, would have found outrageously offensive. Far from greeting his own impending death with stoical aplomb, the thought of it plunges him into a frightful panic in the garden of Gethsemane. On no occasion does he counsel the afflicted to be reconciled to their woes. On the contrary, he seems to grasp the point that the diseased and disabled are prevented from taking their full part in the human community. His aim is to restore them to their full humanity by returning them to the fellowship of society at large.

Jesus is remarkably laid back about sexuality, unlike those millions of his followers who can think of hardly anything else, and who have that much in common with the pornographers they run out of town. In fact, there is hardly anything about sexuality in the New Testament, which is no doubt one reason why the work is not taught in cultural studies courses. At one point, Jesus stops off to chat with a plurally adulterous young Samaritan woman, thus violating three taboos simultaneously for a young holy man of the day: don't talk to women alone, don't talk to women with a disreputable sexual history, and above all don't talk to those low-life creatures known as Samaritans. He does not rebuke her for her colorful past, but offers her instead what he calls the water of life, which she eagerly accepts. He seems to take the point that compulsively sleeping around betrays an inability to live fully.

One might contrast this rather negligent attitude to sexuality with a recent report in the *New York Times* about a Father-Daughter Purity Ball in Colorado.[12] In floor-length gowns and tiaras, seventy or so young women of college age danced with their fathers or future fathers-in-law to the sound of synthesized hymns in a ballroom containing nothing but a seven-foot wooden cross. After dessert, the fathers stood and read out loud a solemn promise that they would "before God cover my daughter as her authority and protection in the area of purity." (The exact meaning of "cover" in this context is left unclear.) The event, which apparently alternated between giddy dancing and Christian ritual, cost $10,000 to stage.

One young woman, the daughter of a man named

Randy, remarked to reporters that what she needed from her father was being told that she was beautiful. "If we don't get it from home," she commented, "we will go out to the culture and get it from them." Once again, the precise meaning of the verb "get it" remains ambiguous. Some of the fathers announced that pledging to protect their daughter's purity made them less likely to cheat on their wives. They were, they observed, "taking a stand" for their families and their nation. From time to time they held their daughters close and whispered a brief prayer, and every half an hour the dance was halted so that the fathers could bless their offspring. At the end of the evening "the fathers took their flushed and sometimes sleepy girls toward the exit. But one father took his two young daughters for a walk around the hotel's dark, glassy lake." It is scandalous that a once-reputable newspaper like the *New York Times* should give space to this barely sublimated orgy of incestuous desire.

Sin, Thomas Aquinas claims, has so distorted our emotional natures that we are unable to enjoy sex as we should.[13] If by sin one means violence, aggression, envy, exploitation, acquisitiveness, possessiveness, and so on, then that these damage our creaturely and affective life can scarcely be denied. All this is what Saint Paul means by the sins of the flesh, which, as the atheistic French philosopher Alain Badiou recognizes, has nothing to do with the supposed badness of the body.[14] It is a myth that Paul was hostile to the body. Despite being a celibate, then, Aquinas is surely right. (It is an empiricist mistake to believe that you have to know about sex firsthand in order to be perceptive about it, just as you do not have to play the fiddle to know when someone is making an appalling mess of Mendelssohn's violin concerto.) Aquinas did not draw a sharp contrast between divine and erotic love: he thought that charity presupposes rather than excludes the erotic.[15]

It is worth adding that Jesus's attitude to the family is one of implacable hostility. He has come to break up these cozy little conservative settlements so beloved of American advertisers in the name of his mission, setting their members at each other's throats; and he seems to have precious little time for his own family in particular. In *The God Delusion,* Richard Dawkins greets this aspect of the Gospel with chilly suburban distaste. Such a cold-eyed view of the family can suggest to him only the kidnapping habits of religious cults. He does not see that movements for justice cut across traditional blood ties, as well as across ethnic, social, and national divisions. Justice is thicker than blood.

One reason why Christianity has proved intuitively attractive to many people is that it places love at the center of its vision of the world—even if, as we have seen, its version of love is peculiarly unlovely. This strikes a lot of people as fairly plausible, given that their experience suggests that love is the most precious of all values. That love is the focal point of human history, though everywhere spurned and denied, has a convincing enough ring to it in one sense. In another sense, however, it is a hard recognition—partly because in reality love is so palpably not the focal point of history, and partly because we live in an age in which it has been effectively privatized, which is no doubt one reason among many why the Christian faith makes no sense to a great many modern men and women.

For the liberal humanist legacy to which Ditchkins is indebted, love can really be understood only in personal terms. It is not an item in his political lexicon, and would sound merely embarrassing were it to turn up there. For the liberal tradition, what seems to many men and women to lie at the core of human existence has a peripheral place in the affairs of the world, however vital a role it may play in the private life. The concept of political love, one imagines, would make little sense to Ditchkins. Yet something like this is the ethical basis for socialism.[16] It is just that it is hard to see what this might mean in a civilization where love has been almost wholly reduced to the erotic, romantic, or domestic. Ditchkins writes as he does partly because a legacy which offers an alternative to the liberal heritage on this question is today in danger of sinking without trace.

Now I would be reluctant to label the account of Christian faith I have just given liberation theology. All authentic theology is liberation theology. Nor am I necessarily proposing it as true, for the excellent reason that it may very well not be. It may be no more plausible than the tooth fairy. I should add, however, that holding views like this is an excellent strategy for anyone wishing to get rid of all their friends and colleagues at a stroke, provoking as they do irritation from the secular left and outrage from the religious right. Left-wing Christians are in dire need of dating agencies. But though the account may not be true, it is not, in my opinion, stupid, vicious, or absurd. And if it evokes no response from Ditchkins at all, then I think his life is the poorer.

Many reflective people these days will see good reason to reject religious belief. But even if the account I have given of it is not literally true, it may still serve as an allegory of our political and historical condition. Besides, critics of the most enduring form of popular culture in human history have a moral obligation to confront that case at its most persuasive, rather than grabbing themselves a victory on the cheap by savaging it as so much garbage and gobbledygook. The mainstream Christian theology I have outlined here may well be false; but anyone who holds to it is in my view deserving of respect. This is not the case for those who champion imperial wars, or who sneer at religion from the Senior Common Room window as yet more evidence of the thick-headedness of the masses. Ditchkins, by contrast, considers that no religious belief, anywhere or anytime, is worthy of any respect whatsoever. And this, one might note, is the opinion of a man deeply averse to dogmatism.

Insofar as the faith I have described is neither stupid nor vicious, then I believe it is worth putting in a word for it against the enormous condescension of those like Ditchkins, who in a fine equipoise of arrogance and ignorance assert that all religious belief is repulsive. That a great deal of it is indeed repulsive, not to speak of nonsensical, is not a bone of contention between us. But I speak here partly in defense of my own forebears, against the charge that the creed to which they dedicated their lives is worthless and void. It is in the spirit of democracy to hold that any doctrine to which many millions of men and women have clung over long periods of time is unlikely to have nothing going for it whatsoever. What it has going for it, to be sure, may not be what those who hold the doctrine consider it to be; but there are many possibilities between this and pure garbage. It ought always to be possible to extract the rational kernel from the mystical shell.[17] I also seek to strike a minor blow on behalf of those many millions of Muslims whose creed of peace, justice, and compassion has been rubbished and traduced by cultural supremacists in the West. We live in an age in which, since 9/11, racism is becoming once more intellectually respectable.

I am not foolish enough to imagine for a moment that Ditchkins would be impressed by the theological account I have given, since for one thing it is scarcely the conventional wisdom of North Oxford or Washington, D.C. It represents a view of the human condition which is far more radical than anything Richard Dawkins is likely to countenance, with his eminently suburban, smugly sanguine trust in the efficacy of a spot of social engineering here and a dose of liberal enlightenment there. (The anti-Enlightenment crew are no more plausible either, as I shall be arguing later on.) The view of the world I have just laid out is not what one characteristically hears around North Oxford dinner tables or in the fleshpots of the U.S. capital.

Hitchens, Martin Amis, Salman Rushdie, Ian McEwan, and other members of the liberal literati have spoken up with admirable eloquence for the value of free expression, against what they rightly denounce as a bigoted and benighted Islamism. This is to be warmly welcomed. But not unequivocally so. For one thing, Rushdie has recently announced that he is now very far from politics—a curious admission, one might think, at a time when his own people are under more ferocious attack in the West, and subject to more withering insult and contempt, than for a very long time. He has also defended Amis's odious recommendations for harassing and discriminating against ordinary Muslims, recorded in an interview after 9/11, as simply giving voice to a public fear, as though Amis were actually performing a valuable public service by his panic-stricken invective. Rushdie also denies that Amis was advocating discrimination at all, despite the fact that the latter speaks in his interview of favoring "discriminatory stuff." Christopher Hitchens has also defended Amis's comments in the blandest conceivable terms as no more than a mind-experiment. It is remarkable how passionate some commentators can be in their disinterested search for justice and true judgment, except when it comes to their friends.

For another thing, is there not something a touch self-interested, as well as commendably principled, about devoting almost the whole of one's political energies to just the kind of issue which touches most on one's own professional situation? What would one say of a trade unionist who was silent on everything but the right to strike, or a feminist who was agitated about abortion but seemed nonchalant about sweated labor?

This is not a criticism which applies to Hitchens, who has always been politically engaged across a broad spectrum of issues. But it certainly applies to some other morally indignant observers today. What is one to make of the tirades of those who appear to know little of politics beyond their own invaluable right to publish their stuff and say what they think? One might claim, to be sure, that poets and novelists have no more special privilege to hand down political judgments than nurses or truck drivers—that their vocation grants them no particular entitlement to be heard on such momentous questions. If they are intent on issuing such pronouncements, however, it is surely preferable that these professional traders in human sympathies should try to look a little beyond their own immediate interests, important though they are.

The antagonism between Ditchkins and those like myself, then, is quite as much political as theological. Where Richard Dawkins and I differ most fundamentally, I suspect, is not on the question of God, science, superstition, evolution, or the origins of the universe. Theologians are not in the least interested qua theologians in, say, whether a process as crude and blundering as evolution could have produced something as exquisitely complex as Henry James. The difference between science and theology, as I understand it, is one over whether you see the world as a gift or not; and you cannot resolve this just by inspecting the thing, any more than you can deduce from examining a porcelain vase that it is a wedding present. The difference between Ditchkins and radicals like myself also hinges on whether it is true that the ultimate signifier of the human condition is the tortured and murdered body of a political criminal, and what the implications of this are for living.

Faith, Ditchkins seems not to register, is not primarily a belief that something or someone exists, but a commitment and allegiance—faith *in* something which might make a difference to the frightful situation you find yourself in, as is the case, say, with faith in feminism or anticolonialism. It is not in the first place a question of signing up to a description of reality, though it certainly involves that as well. Christian faith, as I understand it, is not primarily a matter of signing on for the proposition that there exists a Supreme Being, but the kind of commitment made manifest by a human being at the end of his tether, foundering in darkness, pain, and bewilderment, who nevertheless remains faithful to the promise of a transformative love. The trouble with the Dawkinses of this world, however, is that they do not find themselves in a frightful situation at all (unless, like myself, one counts Oxford

High Table in that category), beyond the fact that there are a lot of semideranged people called believers around the place.

It is natural, then, that they have no use for such embarrassingly old-fashioned ideas as depravity and redemption. Even after Auschwitz, there is nothing in their view to be redeemed from. Things are just not that desperate enough. In their opinion, it is just shoddy, self-indulgent leftist hyperbole to imagine that they are. Your average liberal rationalist does not need to believe that despite the tormented condition of humanity there might still, implausibly enough, be hope, since they do not credit such a condition in the first place. This is one important reason why God-talk makes no sense to them, though it is by no means the only reason. Plenty of people repudiate God for eminently creditable reasons; but as far as this point goes, Ditchkins rejects him for reasons which are both boring and politically disreputable.

As the first truly global mass movement in human history, Christianity finds in what it sees as the coming kingdom of God a condition of justice, fellowship, and self-fulfillment far beyond anything that might normally be considered possible or even desirable in the more well-heeled quarters of Oxford and Washington. It is hard to imagine informing some hard-bitten political lobbyist in a Washington bar that only through a tragic process of loss, nothingness, and self-dispossession can humanity come into its own. In such civilized circles, God-talk is not really any more acceptable than talk about socialism. Neither language game fits at all smoothly into the hard-nosed ethos of contemporary capitalism. When Christopher Hitchens writes in a review of liberation theology as a "sorry" affair, one takes it that he is referring to the liberation quite as much as to the theology. In *God Is Not Great* he even suggests that there were some good reasons for the papacy to put this theological movement down as heretical. It is not often that Christopher Hitchens is to be found defending the pope. But it chimes well enough with his politics. In the so-called Santa Fe document of 1980, the U.S. government denounced such theology as a subversive threat. One gathers from Daniel Dennett's indifferently written, disappointingly conventional critique of religion, *Breaking the Spell,* that he thinks that the invasion of Iraq was fine if it only could have been better managed, which is enough to suggest that not every atheistic iconoclast is radical in any other sense of the word.

The advanced capitalist system is inherently atheistic. It is godless in its actual material practices, and in the values and beliefs implicit in them, whatever some of its apologists might piously aver. As such, it is atheistic in all the wrong ways, whereas Marx and Nietzsche are atheistic in what are by and large the right kinds of ways. A society of packaged fulfillment, administered desire, managerialized politics, and consumerist economics is unlikely to cut to the kind of depth where theological questions can even be properly raised, just as it rules out political and moral questions of a certain profundity. What on earth would be the point of God in such a setup, other than as ideological legitimation, spiritual nostalgia, or a means of private extrication from a valueless world?

One place where so-called spiritual values, driven from the face of a brutally pragmatic capitalism, have taken refuge is New Ageism, which is just the sort of caricature of the spiritual one would expect a materialistic civilization to produce. Rather as those with hearts of stone tend to weep at schmaltzy music, so those who would not recognize a genuine spiritual value if it fell into their laps tend to see the spiritual as spooky, ethereal, and esoteric. This, incidentally, is what Marx had in mind when he wrote of religion as "the heart of a heartless world, the soul of soulless conditions." He meant that conventional religion is the only kind of heart that a heartless world can imagine, rather as embarrassingly broad humor is the only kind of comedy the humorless can appreciate. The religion Marx attacks betrays just the kind of sentimental, disembodied understanding of the spiritual that one would expect from hard-headed materialists.

Romanticism, as Marx himself pointed out, is among other things the flip side of utilitarianism. Those who are in every other way worldly, cynical, and hard-boiled (Hollywood superstars and the like) reveal a truly bottomless gullibility when it comes to spirituality. Nobody is more otherworldly than the worldly, nobody more soft-centered than the hard-nosed. Spiritual matters must naturally be as remote from their lawyers, minders, agents, and hairstylists as one could imagine, in order to provide some fantasy alternative to them.

This is why people who are in every other respect urbane and streetwise believe that affairs on earth are being controlled from an alien spaceship parked behind a cloud. They would probably not believe this if they had only $38 in the bank. Money is a great breeder of unreality. The idea that spirituality is about visiting the sick and fighting injustice would no doubt strike these Kabbalists, necromancers, and chiropractors of the psyche as intolerably prosaic. Even their minders and hairstylists can do that.

It is in just this sense that Karl Marx described religion as "the sigh of the oppressed creature," as well as the soul of soulless conditions.[18] The extraordinary surge of New Age religion in our own time has been of this kind. It offers a refuge from the world, not a mission to transform it. The sigh of the oppressed creature, as opposed to its cry of anger, is merely a pathological symptom of what is awry with us. Like the neurotic symptom for Freud, this kind of religious faith expresses a thwarted desire which it simultaneously displaces. It does not understand that we could live spiritually in any authentic sense of the word only if we were to change materially. Like Romanticism, it is a reaction to a heartless world which stays confined to the sphere of feelings and values. It therefore represents a protest against a spiritual bankruptcy with which it remains thoroughly complicit. Yet such religion is a symptom of discontent even so, however warped and repugnant. Phrases like "the sigh of the oppressed creature," "the heart of a heartless world," and "the soul of soulless conditions" are not for Marx purely pejorative. Religious illusions stand in for more practical forms of protest. They signpost a problem to which they themselves are not the solution.

Islamic radicalism and Christian fundamentalism would seem quite different from this. Unlike Romanticism or New Ageism, they are movements of the masses, not just the doctrines of a disaffected minority. Religion here is less the opium of the people than their crack cocaine. Fundamentalism does indeed set out to change the world rather than simply seek refuge from it. If it rejects the values of modernity, it is quite ready to embrace its technology and forms of organization, whether in the form of chemical warfare or media technology. Those British leftists or former leftists who supported the invasion of Iraq, and who wrote in their manifesto on the subject that "We reject fear of modernity,"[19] were wrong on two counts: Islamism does not reject modernity *tout court,* and in any case there is much in modernity to be rejected. Finding chemical warfare a trifle alarming does not make you a nostalgic reactionary. If this is not to be feared, it is hard to know what is.

In the teeth of what it decries as a hedonistic, relativistic culture, Christian fundamentalism seeks to reinstate order, chastity, thrift, hard work, self-discipline, and responsibility, all values that a godless consumerism threatens to rout. It some ways, its criticisms of the status quo are quite correct, which is what many a good liberal will not allow. Late capitalism does indeed breed a culture of mindless hedonism, sexual obsession, and moral shallowness. It is just that fundamentalism offers a cure which is probably even worse than the sickness. Fundamentalism is otherworldly in the sense that its values spring from an earlier epoch of capitalism (industrial production), not just because it dreams of pie in the sky. It is less the sigh of the oppressed creature than of the ousted one. Fundamentalists are for the most part those whom capitalism has left behind. It has broken faith with them, as it will break faith with anyone and anything that no longer yields it a profit.

Yet if New Ageism is apolitical, Christian fundamentalism is antipolitical. It may be politically militant, but it is basically a form of culturalism, seeking to replace politics with religion. Much the same is true of Al Qaida. Nothing is more antipolitical than planting bombs in public places, even in the name of a political cause. As Gilbert Achcar comments, whereas Christian liberation theology is a component of the political left in general, "Islamic fundamentalism developed in most Muslim-majority countries as a competitor of, and an alternative to, the left—in trying to channel protest against 'real misery,' and the state and society that are held responsible for it."[20] As such, it belongs to an age in which culture betrays a worrying tendency to grow too big for its boots and confiscate the political altogether. There are similar tendencies in so-called identity politics, some of which belong to the same global disillusionment with the political. Islamic radicalism, like Christian fundamentalism, believes in replacing politics with religion. If politics has failed to emancipate you, perhaps religion will fare better. We shall return to this topic at the end of the book.

What is distinctive about our age when it comes to religion, then, is not just that it is everywhere on the rise, from Islamist militancy and Russian Orthodoxy to Pentacostalism and Evangelical Protestantism in Latin America. It is also that this resurgence often seems to take a political form. Yet this reflects a failure of politics proper rather than a reinvigoration of it. Modernity, by and large, is the era in which religion retires from the public sphere in the West to be cultivated as a private pursuit, like troilism or marquetry. If it thus becomes fairly meaningless, the damage it can inflict is at least diminished. Postmodernity is the era in which religion goes public and collective once again, but more as a substitute for classical politics than a reassertion of it. We are witnessing an alarming reenchantment of the late capitalist world—a rekindling of the spiritual aura, so to speak, after an age of mechanical reproduction. This is a religion that is once more prepared to agitate and kill. Perhaps this is also a postnationalist phenomenon. In the epoch of modernity, nationalism, as perhaps the most "poetic" form of politics, provided an outlet for spiritual or symbolic energies which have now been forced to migrate elsewhere. Postmodernism takes off where revolutionary nationalism ends.

What is the postmodern response to the kind of theology I have outlined? The idea of postmodern culture rejecting such theology in some conscious way is absurd. It just doesn't have enough doctrinal consciousness to do so. It no more dismisses theology than it dismisses Swahili or the Antarctic. Such a social order is posttheological only in the sense that Madonna is post-Darwinian. There is a thriving postmodern theology, but it is hardly typical of the culture as a whole. It is unlikely that words like "grace" or "fallenness" or "redemption" can exert much force in a social order where even words like "emancipation" are greeted with bemused silence. Emancipation from what, exactly? Isn't that just too sixties to be true? How could there be a transformed future in a culture for which, as one postmodern thinker excitedly remarked, the future will be the present "only with more options"?

What is the point of faith or hope in a civilization which regards itself as pretty well self-sufficient, as being more or less as good as it gets, or at least as a spectacular advance on what went before? It is hard to see what role faith could play, other than a sheerly ideological one, in a Western world which some of its inhabitants see as nothing less than the very consummation of human history, lacking nothing but more of the same. How could such a form of life accept that there is something profoundly amiss with our condition—that it simply does not add up, that it is in several respects intolerable, and that one of the chief signs of this incoherence and intolerability is the plight of the poor?

To date, capitalism has not abandoned its religious and metaphysical superstructure, whatever it may find itself compelled to do in the future. One would certainly not rule the possibility out, not least if, in a world of terrorism, religious faith becomes increasingly identical with a socially dysfunctional fundamentalism. The problem for the present, not least in the United States, is that religion, as one of the few places in which some of the spiritual values expelled by the marketplace can find shelter, becomes by this very situation defensive, paranoid, and semipathological. Its remoteness from the practical world is one cause of this, as it is one cause of the "pathological" quality of some modernist art. Religion is therefore less and less able to legitimate the social order, with its innately godless priorities. It therefore ceases even to have much of an ideological function, which pushes it further into irrelevance. The social order betrays in its everyday practice that it does not and cannot believe in the spiritual values it supposedly holds dear, whatever it may solemnly claim on Sundays or in presidential addresses to the nation. What it does, and the way it justifies this to itself, are grotesquely at odds with each other. It is a discrepancy between ideal and reality which also applies to a great deal of religion, as we shall now go on to see.

## CHAPTER TWO

# The Revolution Betrayed

The account of Christian faith I have just outlined is one which I take to be thoroughly orthodox, scriptural, and traditional. There is nothing fashionable or newfangled about it; indeed, much of it goes back to Aquinas and beyond. In my view, it is a lot more realistic about humanity than the likes of Dawkins. It takes the full measure of human depravity and perversity, in contrast to what we shall see later to be the extraordinarily Pollyannaish view of human progress of *The God Delusion*. At the same time, it is a good deal bolder than the liberal humanists and rationalists about the chances of this dire condition being repaired. It is more gloomy in its view of the human species than the *bien-pensant* liberal intelligentsia (only Freudianism or the philosophy of Arthur Schopenhauer can match it here), and certainly a good deal more skeptical than the naïve upbeatness of American ideology, which tends to mistake a hubristic cult of can-do-ery for the virtue of hope. (A nation which can even contemplate replacing the World Trade Center with an even taller building is clearly something of a slow learner, and not just from the viewpoint of homeland security.) Yet it also believes that the very frailty of the human can become a redemptive power. In this, it is at one with socialism, for which the harbingers of a future social order are those who have little to lose in the present.

Christianity believes that a great deal of human wickedness is historically caused, and can be tackled by political action. But it also thinks it wildly implausible, given the scale and persistence of human viciousness, to think that this is all there is to the matter—that there are not flaws and contradictions built into the structure of the human species itself, which cannot simply be historicized away. Psychoanalysis holds much the same view. There has been no human culture to date in which virtue has been predominant. Some of the reasons for this are alterable, while others are probably not. This is not to conclude that racism or sexism or capitalism cannot be defeated, but simply to take a sober measure of the difficulties involved in such a project. Yet at the same time Christian faith is absurdly, outrageously more hopeful than liberal rationalism, with its apparently unhinged belief that not only is the salvation of the human species possible but that, contrary to all we read in the newspapers, it has in principle already taken place. Not even the most rose-tinted Trotskyist believes that.

A huge number of the charges that Ditchkins levels against actually existing religion are thoroughly justified, and he deserves a great deal of credit for parading them so forcefully. Indeed, it is hard to imagine how any polemic against, say, the clerical abuse of children or the religious degradation of women could be too severe or exaggerated. Yet it is scarcely a novel point to claim that for the most part Ditchkins holds forth on religion in truly shocking ignorance of many of its tenets—a situation I have compared elsewhere to the arrogance of one who regards himself as competent to pronounce on arcane questions of biology on the strength of a passing acquaintance with the *British Book of Birds*.[1] Some might claim in defense of Ditchkins that he is speaking of religion as a social phenomenon, not of theology; but how could you speak of, say, fascism as a social phenomenon without a reasonably accurate grasp of its teachings? As Denys Turner remarks, "It is indeed extraordinary how theologically stuck in their ways some atheists are."[2] Stephen Mulhall writes in a similar vein of "the atheist's superstitious conception of God."[3] An atheist who has more than a primitive (one might say Satanic) understanding of theology is as rare as an American who has not been abducted by aliens.

The truth is that a good many secular intellectuals with

a reasonably sophisticated sense of what goes on in academic areas other than their own tout an abysmally crude, infantile version of what theology has traditionally maintained. These days, theology is the queen of the sciences in a rather less august sense of the word "queen" than in its medieval heyday. These intellectuals claim as Christian doctrine the idea that God is some sort of superentity outside the universe; that he created the world rather as a carpenter might fashion a stool; that faith in this God means above all subscribing to the proposition that he exists; that there is a real me inside me called the soul, which a wrathful God may consign to hell if I am not egregiously well-behaved; that our utter dependency on this deity is what stops us thinking and acting for ourselves; that this God cares deeply about whether we are sinful or not, because if we are then he demands to be placated, and other such secular fantasies.

With dreary predictability, Daniel C. Dennett defines religions at the beginning of his *Breaking the Spell* as "social systems whose participants avow belief in a supernatural agent or agents whose approval is to be sought,"[4] which as far as Christianity goes is rather like beginning a history of the potato by defining it as a rare species of rattlesnake. Predictably, Dennett's image of God is a Satanic one. He also commits the Ditchkins-like blunder of believing that religion is a botched attempt to explain the world, which is like seeing ballet as a botched attempt to run for a bus. Hitchens, too, writes in Satanic style of God as an angry, jealous, blood-loving being who teaches men and women to feel worthless. The Almighty in his view is a kind of cosmic version of the CIA, keeping us under constant surveillance.

When people like this are told that these are crude distortions of Christian belief, they imagine that this means not that they never were orthodox doctrine, but that they have been ditched in the modern age by a clutch of guitar-toting liberal revisionists. As far as theology goes, Ditchkins has an enormous amount in common with Ian Paisley and American TV evangelists. Both parties agree pretty much on what religion consists in; it is just that Ditchkins rejects it while Pat Robertson and his unctuous crew grow fat on it. There are always topics on which otherwise scrupulous minds will cave in to the grossest prejudice with hardly a struggle. For most academic psychologists, it is Jacques Lacan; for Oxbridge philosophers it is Heidegger or Sartre; for former citizens of the Soviet bloc it is Marx; for militant atheists it is religion.

It is, in fact, entirely logical that those who see religion as nothing but false consciousness should so often get it wrong, since what profit is to be reaped from the meticulous study of a belief system you hold to be as pernicious as it is foolish? Who is likely to launch a time-consuming investigation of what Kabbalists, occultists, or Rosicrucians actually hold, when there is still *War and Peace* to be read and the children to be put to bed? So it is that those who polemicize most ferociously against religion regularly turn out to be the least qualified to do so, rather as many of those who polemicize against literary theory do not hate it because they have read it, but rather do not read it because they hate it. It is as though when it comes to religion—the single most powerful, pervasive, persistent form of popular culture human history has ever witnessed, as well as in many respects one of the most obnoxious—any old travesty will do. And this view is often shared by those ebulliently on the side of the common people.

In a similar way, when it comes to the political left, no blow is too low, no libel too crass, no slur too scabrous for certain of their antagonists, among whom we are now forced to include the more bibulous half of Ditchkins. When it comes to God, liberal rationalists who are otherwise accustomed to enforcing fine discriminations are permitted, agreeably enough, to be as sloppy and raucous as they please. In the face of so-called irrationalism, science yields to stridency with hardly a struggle. Like the so-called war on terror, such rationalism is in danger of mimicking the "irrationalism" it confronts in the very act of seeking to resist it.

This straw-targeting of Christianity is now drearily commonplace among academics and intellectuals—that is to say, among those who would not allow a first-year student to get away with the vulgar caricatures in which they themselves indulge with such insouciance. Ditchkins on theology is rather like someone who lays claim to the title of literary criticism by commenting that there are some nice bits in the novel and some scary bits as well, and it's all very sad at the end. He thinks, for example, that all Christians are fideists, holding that reason is irrelevant to faith, which is rather like believing that all Scots are stingy. (Ludwig Wittgenstein, incidentally, had the rare distinction of being a fideist without being a believer.) Hitchens's *God Is Not Great* is littered with elementary theological howlers. We learn that the God of the Old Testament never speaks of solidarity and compassion; that Christ has no human nature; and that the doctrine of the resurrection means that he did not die. In a passage of surreally potted history, Hitchens seems to hold the obscure Jewish sect of the second-century BC known as the Maccabees responsible not only for the emergence of Christianity but also for the advent of Islam. It is surprising that he does not pin Stalinism on them as well. For his part, Dawkins seems to believe that Paul was the author of the epistle to the Hebrews, and that to say that Jesus was the son of God means that he was omniscient. The sagacious advice to know your enemy is cavalierly set aside. The Frank Kermodes of this world are rare indeed.[5]

*God Is Not Great* is also a fine illustration of how atheistic fundamentalists are in some ways the inverted mirror image of Christian ones. And not just in their intemperate zeal and tedious obsessiveness. Hitchens argues earnestly that the Book of Genesis doesn't mention marsupials; that the Old Testament Jews surely couldn't have wandered for forty years in the desert; that the capture of the huge bedstead of the giant Og, king of Bashan, might never have occurred at all, and so on. This is rather like someone vehemently trying to convince you, with fastidious attention to architectural and zoological detail, that King Kong could not possibly have scaled the Empire State Building because it would have collapsed under his weight. This is not to relegate the Bible as a whole to the realm of myth, poetry, and fiction, thus shielding it conveniently from rational or historical investigation. It is simply to indicate that the relations between these domains and historical fact in Scripture are exceedingly complex, and that on this score as on many another, Hitchens is hair-raisingly ignorant of generations of modern biblical scholarship.

Elsewhere in his book he decries the religious attempt "to assert the literal and limited mind over the ironic and inquiring one" (259). Given that he argues for much of the time on the same level as the fundamentalists, the difference lying mainly in the point of view, it is all too obvious on what side of his own divide he falls. For much of the time the liberal ironist yields without a struggle to the heavy-handed positivist. Fundamentalism is in large part a failure of the imagination, and in his treatment of Scripture (as opposed, say, to his reading of George Orwell or Saul Bellow), Hitchens's imagination fails catastrophically. Like Dawkins, he fails to grasp the nature of a theological claim. He is like an incompetent literary critic who rips the sleepwalking scene in *Macbeth* from the whole intricate context of the drama and asks us exasperatedly whether on earth it is probable. Which is not to imply that Christians regard their Gospel as a fiction. Indeed, that simple-minded opposition is itself part of the problem.

Yet it is most certainly Christianity itself which is primarily responsible for the intellectual sloppiness of its critics. Apart from the signal instance of Stalinism, it is hard to think of a historical movement that has more squalidly betrayed its own revolutionary origins. Christianity long ago shifted from the side of the poor and dispossessed to that of the rich and aggressive. The liberal Establishment really has little to fear from it and everything to gain. For the most part, it has become the creed of the suburban well-to-do, not the astonishing promise offered to the riffraff and undercover anti-colonial militants with whom Jesus himself hung out. The suburbanite response to the *anawim,* a term which can be roughly translated into American English as "loser," is for the most part to flush them off the streets.

This brand of piety is horrified by the sight of a female breast, but considerably less appalled by the obscene inequalities between rich and poor. It laments the death of a fetus, but is apparently undisturbed by the burning to death of children in Iraq or Afghanistan in the name of U.S. global dominion. By and large, it worships a God fashioned blasphemously in its own image—a clean-shaven, short-haired, gun-toting, sexually obsessive God with a special regard for that ontologically privileged piece of the globe just south of Canada and north of Mexico, rather than the Yahweh who is homeless, faceless, stateless, and imageless, who prods his people out of their comfortable settlement into the trackless terrors of the desert, and who brusquely informs them that their burnt offerings stink in his nostrils. One is told that there is an American prayer "for High Achievers," in which God is said to be "the greatest achiever of all." In fact, the only one of his achievements we can actually see with our eyes is the world; and if this is the best he can do, one is distinctly underwhelmed by his talents.

Far from refusing to conform to the powers of this world, Christianity has become the nauseating cant of lying politicians, corrupt bankers, and fanatical neocons, as well as an immensely profitable industry in its own right. There is a company in the United States today which for an annual subscription will automatically send off e-mail messages to your faithless friends and colleagues when Christ comes again, pleading with them for a last-minute conversion before you yourself are "raptured" into heaven and they are left stranded on earth. Probably no nation on earth has plucked such a farrago of superstitious nonsense from the New Testament as the United States, with its incurable talent for going over the top.

The Christian church has tortured and disemboweled in the name of Jesus, gagging dissent and burning its critics alive. It has been oily, sanctimonious, brutally oppressive, and vilely bigoted. Morality for this brand of belief is a matter of the bedroom rather than the boardroom. It supports murderous dictatorships in the name of God, views both criticism and pessimism as unpatriotic, and imagines that being a Christian means maintaining a glazed grin, a substantial bank balance, and a mouthful of pious platitudes. It denounces terrorism, but excludes from its strictures such kidnapping, torturing, murdering outfits as the CIA. (One CIA intervention which has not received the urgent attention it merits, by the way, was the agency's dissemination of a Russian translation of T. S. Eliot's *The Waste Land* during the Cold War. Was this to demonstrate the virtues of both free verse and free expression, or to demoralize the Soviets by unleashing the virus of nihilism into their midst?)

This brand of faith fails to see that the only cure for terrorism is justice. It also fails to grasp to what extent the hideous, disfigured thing clamoring at its gates is its own monstrous creation. It is unable to acknowledge this thing of darkness as in part its own, unable to find its own reflection in its distorted visage. In the light of all this, the bellicose ravings of Ditchkins are, if anything, too muted. It is hard to avoid the feeling that a God as bright, resourceful, and imaginative as the one that might just possibly exist could not have hit on some more agreeable way of saving the world than religion.

I am talking, then, about the distinction between what seems to me a scriptural and an ideological kind of Christian faith—a distinction which can never simply be assumed but must be interminably argued. One name for this thankless exercise is what Nietzsche, who held that churches were the tombs and sepulchres of God, called in Kierkegaardian phrase saving Christianity from Christendom. Any preaching of the Gospel which fails to constitute a scandal and affront to the political state is in my view effectively worthless. It is not a project which at present holds out much promise of success. Yet it is from the standpoint of values which spring among other places from the Judeo-Christian legacy itself that we identify these failings in the churches—just as liberal civilization is, so to speak, its own immanent critique, as a culture which allows us to castigate its shortcomings by reference to its own commendably high standards.

Even so, it might well be objected that the account of Christian faith I have sketched here is the product of an intellectual elite loftily remote from actually existing religion. This is what one might call the populist argument from the Person in the Pew. It is of course true that there is a gap between a sophisticated theological understanding of the Christian Gospel, and the faith of millions of men and women who have neither the leisure nor the education for such scholarly inquiries. Much the same gap yawns between Dawkins and your average believer in evolution, or between Islamic theology and those deluded Islamic radicals who are profoundly ignorant of their own faith. It is true that a great many Christians have fallen prey to flagrantly ideological versions of the Gospel—that is to say, versions of it which in one way or another play into the hands of what Saint John darkly refers to as the powers of this world. As far as I can see, there is no support in Scripture for what I believe may still be the practice at the Mormons' Brigham Young University (I refrain from placing that last word in scare quotes), where those students or faculty members who need for medical reasons to grow beards are required to carry on their persons a so-called beard card. But perhaps I have overlooked some vital antishaving verse in Luke or Matthew here.

It is not in fact the case that this understanding of the Gospel is confined to an intellectual elite. My own father, who left school at the age of fifteen to work as a manual laborer in a factory, and who scarcely read a book in his life, would, I am sure, have endorsed it. Similarly, those on the political left who regard socialism as more than just a matter of labor camps and mass murder are not simply a cerebral coterie who happen to be familiar with the intricacies of the *Grundrisse.* On the contrary, hundreds of thousands of rank-and-file members of the working-class movement have rejected such claims (claims themselves, as it happens, generally made by an intellectual coterie) for some more authentic version of socialism. There is no reason to think anything different of the Christian movement. In any case, you do not settle the question of whether, say, the New Testament is on the side of the rich and powerful by appealing to what most people happen to believe, any more than you verify the Second Law of Thermodynamics by popular acclaim. You simply have to argue the question on the evidence as best you can.

Those who dismiss what I would see as soundly based readings of the Gospel because they are not always widely shared among Christians are rather like those who object to some soundly based doctrines of liberalism simply because a lot of ordinary men and women believe in electrocuting pedophiles and shipping immigrants back to where they came from. But not all of them do. Ordinary people who say things like "It'd be a funny world if we all thought the same" or "It takes all kinds to make a world" (a tag, incidentally, which struck Ludwig Wittgenstein as "a most beautiful and kindly saying") may not be all that well-versed in John Locke or John Stuart Mill; but this does not mean that they are fascist beasts either. Or at least most of them are not.

Besides, if religion has so flagrantly failed to live up to its own founding principles, what about liberalism? What of the middle-class liberal or Enlightenment lineages which Ditchkins so zealously champions? Have these not been a little less than perfect in their fidelity to their own admirable doctrines? What of the violent suborning of freedom and democracy abroad, the misery wreaked by racism and sexism, the sordid history of colonialism and imperialism, the generation of poverty and famine, the warfare and genocide of sublime proportions, the arming and championing of one odious tyrant after another? What human carnage terrorism has so far murderously wreaked in the West is minor indeed compared to the long history of slaughter and oppression of the West itself. It is true that we do not know what the future may hold in this respect. But it would take even the most resolute of terrorists a very long time indeed to rival the barbarous record of Western warfare and imperialism. It is quite as probable that we in the more prosperous sector of the world will be done in by our own internecine quarrels as that we shall be done away with by the new narrative of terrorism. Most of those Western commentators who have greeted the crimes of Islamic terrorism with panic and hysteria have not shouted quite so loudly about the long catalogue of atrocities of their own supposedly enlightened civilization. Why was it only after 9/11, when they themselves became for the first time potential victims of attack, that their moral indignation broke cover so stridently? There is nothing wrong with protesting against bloodthirsty bigots who seek to deprive you of your limbs, as long as you have the elementary sense of justice to point out that one major reason for this criminal intent is the shameful way the West has treated others in the past.

That many in the United States learned absolutely nothing from the onslaughts of 9/11 is clear enough from Susan Faludi's brave study *The Terror Dream: What 9/11 Revealed About America.* 9/11, Faludi argues, was a crisis of American virility from which the nation very quickly recovered. Only weeks after the attack, George Bush called on a clutch of Hollywood moguls to help market the war on terror; and part of the project was to herald the return of traditional American manliness after what one writer quoted by Faludi called the "pussification of the American man." Under the emasculating influence of feminism, American males had grown flabby and gelded, shaved-and-waxed male bimbos whose limp-wristed lifestyle had laid the nation open to the Islamicist assault. The phallic symbol of America had been cut off, one blogger fantasized, and at its base was a large, smoldering vagina. "Well, this sure pushes feminism off the map!" was one U.S. reporter's response to the loss of three thousand lives. A *Band of Brothers* ethic, so one news magazine put it, could not take root in a female-obsessed *Sex and the City* culture. The U.S. had lost its balls along with its immunity to foreign invasion. A nation that had traditionally had some difficulty in distinguishing fantasy from reality was now busy conflating the two at every turn.

The aftermath of 9/11, so Faludi reports, witnessed a vicious lampooning of U.S. feminists. The Taliban's oppression of women, much touted for a while, began to evaporate as a cause for concern as the bombs fell on Afghanistan. Meanwhile, squint-eyed Donald Rumsfeld was being celebrated as "the Stud," "a babe magnet," and—such are the egregious illusions of ideology—"the sexiest man alive." Square-jawed, short-haired, gun-toting America, thrust into neurotic self-doubt by an army of castrating bitches, had finally come out of hiding, beating its collective chest. Not long after the attack, men's fashions began to favor hard-hat, military chic and firefighters' jackets. The wide-eyed United States, unlike endemically cynical Europe, has always felt a hunger for heroes, and having an aircraft slam into your office somehow turned you into one.

Or if that was a hard one to argue, there were always the New York firefighters. The grim truth about 9/11, Faludi claims, is that the death toll would have been considerably lower had the firefighters not been sent into the World Trade Center. About three times more firefighters than office workers died on the floors below the impact of the aircraft. But in they were sent anyway, and the media response was to make Sir Galahads of them all. One demented U.S. journal raved that the New York Fire Department were heroes in possession of godlike prowess, beneficence, and divinity. Many of the firefighters themselves begged leave to demur. The fact that they died partly because their radios were not working was swept decorously under the carpet.

It was not long before the firefighters were erotic figures as well as heroic ones. A lust-for-firemen trend was launched. "Firefighters Are a Hot Commodity in the Dating Game!" shrieked one newspaper headline. Women painted their toenails fire-engine red. All this was seen less as kinkiness or hysteria than as a welcome return to sexual normality. The presence of women helping at Ground Zero was coolly ignored. Instead, there was a morbid cult of 9/11 widows, glossily packaged victims who were required to stick submissively to a script written for them by the media. Those who rebelled against their all-American-housewife image were instantly suppressed. A non-victim called Jessica Lynch was non-saved by U.S. soldiers in a non-heroic non-event. Terrorism and domesticity were closely twined: the point of killing Iraqis was to protect your kids. "Goodbye, Soccer Mom, Hello, Security Mom," announced *Time* magazine, maintaining that the terrorist offensive had shocked Americans into a new faith in their oldest values. Everywhere you looked, people were trying to scramble their way back into the womb. A neurotic desire for security gripped a nation newly conscious of its mortality. Women who had ranked their careers over marriage were said bitterly to regret their blunder. The cozy and connubial were in vogue once again. Who, after all, was going to hold your hand when the next blast came?

Some of the actual victims of 9/11, including firefighters, spoke not in the hubristic language of their leaders, but of bonds forged by the shared experience of weakness, fear, and vulnerability. Meanwhile, the Babel-like response of their masters was to consider building an edifice at Ground Zero even higher than the Twin Towers. The grim news was that the United States's moment of tragic crisis was in no way a spiritual conversion. On the contrary, it was business as usual, only a good deal more so.

Ditchkins and his ilk support, by and large, the political status quo, with varying degrees of reformist dissent. He would approve of the first word of the title of this book, but not of the second two. Indeed, Richard Dawkins's swinging assaults on religion, a case of Evangelical atheism if ever there was one, are in marked contrast with the sedate North Oxfordism of his general outlook. (I should point out that I use the term "North Oxford" in an ideological rather than geographical sense. Dawkins may be relieved to learn that I don't actually know where he lives.) His campaign against fundamentalism has been signally unmatched by an equally forthright critique of global capitalism, a system which breeds so much of the anxiety and sense of humiliation off which fundamentalism feeds.

Dawkins dislikes what has flowed from Abraham for some excellent reasons; but he also finds it repugnant for much the same reasons that one can imagine him harboring stoutly Anglo-Saxon objections to Lacan, Situationism, agitprop, Trotsky, Dadaism, the unconscious, Julia Kristeva, Irish republicanism, and allowing one's children to run naked around the garden smoking dope. All of these, one suspects, would be as distasteful to his brisk, bloodless rationality as the Virgin Birth. Jesus is an extremist, as Ditchkins is not. One cannot imagine Ditchkins describing the capitalist system as "almost unequivocally demonic," words used of it by the greatest twentieth-century theologian, Karl Barth.[6]

Ditchkins, in short, is not just a liberal rationalist, but a readily identifiable kind of English middle-class liberal rationalist. Dawkins in particular occasionally writes as though "Thou still unravish'd bride of quietness" is a mighty funny way to describe a Grecian urn. His God-hating is by no means the view of a dispassionate scientist commendably cleansed of prejudice. There is no such animal in any case. It belongs to a specific cultural context. The secular version of the Ten Commandments which he commends to us in *The God Delusion,* one of which counsels us to enjoy our sex lives as long as they don't damage others, are for the most part an assortment of bland liberal platitudes. They can be contrasted in this respect with "Honor your father and your mother," which some Old Testament scholars take to refer not to one's parents but to the old and useless of the tribe who can no longer labor. Or "Do not steal," which in the judgment of some commentators refers not to private property (there was little enough of that around the place) but to the ancient practice of kidnapping the young men of other tribes for their labor power. Or "Keep holy the Sabbath day," which refers not to going to church but the need for a break from the burden of labor. It is a kind of early health-and-welfare requirement. Or "Thou shalt not commit adultery," which warns us not to exploit our sexual charm to break up other people's relationships. The Commandments, writes Herbert McCabe, "tell us to abandon the gods and live in righteousness, in friendship and justice with one another."[7]

Even so, it is perfectly proper and entirely self-consistent for a liberal like Dawkins to oppose *neo*liberalism (he is a stout critic of current U.S. foreign policy), just as one can be a fan of the New Testament but not of the Vatican. Ditchkins rightly upholds liberal values while rejecting quite a few aspects of actually existing liberalism. There is nothing wrong with that. It simply means that he is not in much of a position on this score to call the religious kettle black. Hitchens, we may confidently assume, does not recognize his beloved Jefferson in Guantanamo Bay, however pally he may be with some of the architects of that hellhole. It is just that neither he nor Dawkins shows the same capacity to think both sides of the question simultaneously (which is not at all the same thing as being impeccably even-handed) when it comes to religion. It is here that the liberal rationalism which motivates their aversion to religion suddenly deserts them.

The political left, too, has scarcely been a stranger to the discrepancy between noble ideals and their unsavory incarnation, a fact which somewhat blunts the edge of its protest against religion. It is intriguing, incidentally, that while the left does not appear to object overmuch to Jewish theology (Benjamin, Bloch, Adorno, and the like), or even to, say, Buddhist pacifism, it has an aversion to the Christian brand of belief. Perhaps antireligiousness begins at home. Marxism began among other things as a response to a Christian movement which had betrayed its origins, and ended up in a whole sector of the globe doing much the same. It is just that for the deepest understanding of how and why this happened, and how it might be prevented from happening again, one has to go to certain mainstream currents of Marxism itself. Liberal humanism is simply not radical enough for the purpose. In a similar way, the disgusting betrayals of the Christian churches stand, as we have suggested, under the judgment of the Gospel itself.

One should note that what counts as an "Enlightenment" view is far from obvious. Francis Bacon was an enthusiast of magic, David Hume was a prominent Enlightenment figure with a deep skepticism of reason, Newton dabbled in alchemy, while Voltaire believed in God. Even so, the story of liberal Enlightenment is one of an exhilarating emancipation which constitutes a legacy beyond price. No thinker was more tenaciously of this opinion than Karl Marx. In fact, Hannah Arendt, who was not exactly a socialist, once remarked that her chief complaint against Marx was his admiration for capitalism.[8] (I take it that an enlightened liberalism was one of the great achievements of early capitalist Europe.) The values of the Enlightenment, many of them Judeo-Christian in origin, should be defended against the pretentious follies of postmodernism, and protected, by all legitimate force if necessary, from those high-minded zealots who seek to blow the heads off small children in the name of Allah. Some on the political left, scandalously, have muted their criticisms of such atrocities in their eagerness to point the finger of blame at their own rulers, and should be brought to book for this hypocrisy.

The Enlightenment was deeply shaped by values which stemmed from the Christian tradition. But it was also right, as Ditchkins argues, to see actually existing religion as part of the barbarism and despotism it sought to face down. Even so, in a choice irony, it inherited its brave campaign against superstition partly from Christianity itself, with its rejection of all false gods and prophets, all idols, fetishes, magical rituals, and powers of darkness, in the name of human flesh and blood. It goes without saying that we owe to the Enlightenment freedom of thought, feminism, socialism, humanitarianism, many of our civil liberties, and much of our republican and democratic heritage.

At the same time, this enlightened liberal humanism served as the legitimating ideology of a capitalist culture more steeped in blood than any other episode in human history. This, one may note, is what Ditchkins unaccountably forgets to say. Only Marxism recounts the story of how these two contrasting narratives are secretly one. It reminds us of the mighty achievements of Francis Bacon, but also of the fact that he believed in torture. It insists that modernity means both contraception and Hiroshima, liberation movements and biological warfare. Some people think it Eurocentric to point out that Europe was the historical home of modernity, forgetful that this also means that it was also the home of the Holocaust. The radical answer to the question of whether modernity is a positive or negative phenomenon is an emphatic yes and no. One of the best reasons in my view for still being a Marxist, apart from the gratifying exasperation it sometimes occasions to others, is that no other doctrine I know of claims that the liberal Enlightenment that Ditchkins champions has been at one and the same time an enthralling advance in humanity and an insupportable nightmare—the latter tale, moreover, as verso of the recto of the former, the two colliding histories structurally complicit rather than contingently cheek by jowl.

It is thus that Marxists are able to speak out of both sides of their mouth at the same time. What they have to say yields no comfort to the elegiac gloom of those enemies of Enlightenment (whether patrician and postmodern) for whom, so it would seem, the invention of everything from combine harvesters and dental anesthetics to feminism and the fight for colonial emancipation was a ghastly mistake. At the same time, Marxists cast a cold eye on the kind of progressivist euphoria, of which Dawkins (a spiritual child of H. G. Wells and C. P. Snow) is so resplendent an example, for which, apart from the odd, stubbornly lingering spot of barbarism here and there, history as a whole is still steadily on the up. If ever there was a pious myth and piece of credulous superstition, it is the liberal-rationalist belief that, a few hiccups apart, we are all steadily en route to a finer world. This brittle triumphalism is a hangover from the heroic epoch of liberalism, when the middle classes' star was in the ascendant. Today, it sits cheek by jowl with the cynicism, skepticism, or nihilism into which much of that honorable lineage has degenerated. Radicals are those who believe that things are extremely bad with us, but that they could be feasibly much improved; conservatives believe that things are pretty bad with us but that that's just the way it is with the human animal; and liberals believe that there's a little bit of good and bad in us all.

As Dan Hind argues, the chief threat to enlightened values today springs not from feng shui, faith healing, post-modern relativism, or religious fundamentalism.[9] As usual, it springs from some of the fruits of Enlightenment itself, which has always been its own worst enemy. The language of Enlightenment has been hijacked in the name of corporate greed, the police state, a politically compromised science, and a permanent war economy. The economic individualism of the early, enlightened middle classes has now spawned into vast corporations which trample over group and individual rights, shaping our destinies without the slightest popular accountability. The liberal state, founded among other things to protect individual freedom, has burgeoned in our time into the surveillance state. Scientific rationality and freedom of inquiry have been harnessed to the ends of commercial profit and weapons of war. One vital reason why the United States has declared an open-ended war on terror is to ensure a flow of open-ended profits for a large number of its corporations. An enlightened trust in dispassionate reason has declined to the hiring of scholars and experts to disseminate state and corporate propaganda. Freedom of cultural expression has culminated in the schlock, ideological rhetoric, and politically managed news of the profit-driven mass media.

Rational or enlightened self-interest brings in its wake the irrationality of waste, unemployment, obscene inequalities, manipulative advertising, the accumulation of capital for its own sake, and the dependence of whole livelihoods on a random fluctuation of the market. It also brings with it colonialism and imperialism, which scarcely sit easily with enlightened values. Political individualism, intended to safeguard us from the insolence of power, results in a drastic atrophying of social solidarities. The vital Enlightenment project of controlling Nature, which frees us from being the crushed and afflicted victims of our environment, has resulted in the wholesale pollution of the planet. In claiming the world as our own, we find that we have ended up possessing a lump of dead matter. In asserting our free spirits, we have reduced our own bodies to pieces of mechanism.

The doctrine of universality, which in its heyday meant that everyone had a right to be heard whoever they were, means for some that the West itself is the sole bearer of universal values. The brave vision of internationalism has been largely ousted by the concept of globalization, meaning the right of capital to exercise its sovereign power wherever and over whomever it chooses. Equality comes to mean among other, finer things the equal opportunity to outdo or exploit others in the marketplace. A bracing critique of myth and superstition degenerates into a bloodless scientism for which nothing that cannot be poked and prodded in the laboratory need be taken seriously. The Kantian imperative to have the courage to think for oneself has involved a contemptuous disregard for the resources of tradition and an infantile view of authority as inherently oppressive.

There is another sense, too, in which the values of Enlightenment have ended up at odds with themselves. It is that the act of defending them has been at times indistinguishable from the act of flouting them. To save us from a communism which would confiscate our freedoms, the West has sponsored one vilely autocratic regime after another. In order that Islamist terror should not undermine American civil liberties, the United States has thrown its weight behind the crushing of such liberties in Saudi Arabia, Uzbekistan, Pakistan, and a range of other malodorous regimes. It also seems intent on driving such liberties out of its own homeland. The surest safeguard for freedom in this Orwellian world would seem the training of death squads and the arming of dictators. The United States has a long-standing policy of supporting theocratic monarchies in the name of life, liberty, and the pursuit of happiness. The forces of the Christian right, far from constituting a minor swamp of irrationalism awaiting its moment to be mopped up by the irresistible advance of Reason, have become integral to the workings of the U.S. political system, in a squalid alliance of preachers, lobbyists, businessmen, televangelists, Washington power-brokers, and right-wing politicians.

None of this is to suggest that Enlightenment has had its day. Far from it. Its values are still alive and kicking, despite the worst that some of their supposed patrons can do. Freedom of expression and inquiry, humanitarian sympathies, internationalism, equality of being, open government, the struggle against benighted forms of authoritarianism, and a hunger for political emancipation: these have not withered from the face of the earth, despite the most robust efforts of the liberal-capitalist system which officially lives by such values. That the system has preserved so many of these precious goods, tattered but still intact, is testimony to its resourcefulness and goodwill. That it has protected them from a series of ferocious onslaughts from outside, all the way from fascism to terrorism, is equally to its credit. It is the enemy within which is proving rather more of a problem. Liberal-capitalist cultures inevitably give birth to ills which undermine their own values.

This vital contradiction cannot be grasped as long as irrationalism is always seen as a feature of the Other. Dividing the world between the reasonable and unreasonable, which tends nowadays to coincide rather conveniently with the axis of West and East, overlooks the fact that capitalism breeds irrationalism as predictably as extraterrestrial aliens turn out to be grotesque but easily recognizable versions of ourselves. It is not simply, as Ditchkins seems comfortingly to imagine, that there are still pockets of benightedness within an enlightened world. Benightedness is far closer to the bone than that. The choice between West and East is sometimes one between which particular squalid bunch of murderous fanatics one prefers to back. And this, one would have thought, might be the occasion for a humility and self-criticism for which Ditchkins's writing is not exactly remarkable.

The Whiggish Ditchkins assigns religion to an early, infantile stage of humanity, one which has disastrously outstayed its welcome. With suave patronage, Hitchens relegates religious faith to what he calls "pre-history" or "the childhood of our species" (64), as a brake on what one might see as an otherwise inevitable progress. At stake here is a stupendously simple-minded, breathtakingly reductive world picture, one worthy of a child's crude drawing. There is something striving to move forward, and something intent on holding it back; and while the former is unequivocally good, the second is unreservedly abhorrent. The point is to shake off the lingering remnants of superstition and leap bravely forward into high Victorian rationalism. Hitchens, whose expensive private education peeps out in his sniffy use of the word "hovels," as well as in his withering description of the authors of the Bible as "crude, uncultured human mammals" (102), is loftily condescending about the past as well as about the East. His cultural supremacism extends backward to Democritus as well as sideways to Islam.

In a casual cosmopolitan sneer, Hitchens writes off the offspring of antiquity as "provincials." Religion, he observes in the forward-looking spirit of Feuerbach, Auguste Comte, and Herbert Spencer, springs from the "bawling and fearful infancy of our species," a time in which "nobody . . . had the smallest idea what was going on" (64). One trusts that he does not include Aeschylus in this supercilious dismissal. Saint Paul, speaking of the revolutionary transition from the regime of Law (childlike) to the order of grace (adult), regards faith in Christ as a mature abandoning of infantile idols and superstitions. Paul may well have had the mind of a toddler, indeed in Hitchens's estimate must have had. But his literary works betray surprisingly little hint of it.

In his magisterial study *A Secular Age,* Charles Taylor definitively refutes the well-thumbed myth, wondrous in its simple-minded linearity, that in the course of human affairs a religious view of the world was put to flight by a steady accumulation of scientific evidence. In this flattened, off-the-peg teleology, an Age of Faith is heroically ousted by an Age of Reason. It is one of the plentiful myths or superstitions of Enlightenment. For one thing, Taylor points out, the new, mechanistic science of the seventeenth century was not by and large viewed as a threat to God. In early modern times, scientists were frequently defenders of religious orthodoxy. Deism was one strategy for allowing science and religion to coexist. Faith and Enlightenment were never simple opposites. In the nineteenth century, one of the most unlovely strains of religious belief, Evangelical Christianity, was hottest in the pursuit of the emancipation of slaves.

There was no royal road, then, from the natural sciences to godlessness. The emergent interest in Nature was not a step outside a religious outlook, but a mutation within it. "The pure face-off between 'religion' and 'science,'" Taylor maintains, "is a chimaera, or, rather, an ideological construct."[10] Modern science's portrait of reality is indeed on the whole greatly more accurate than that of premodern myth, even if a great many once-productive scientific hypotheses have been shown up as badly holed. But as Claude Lévi-Strauss shows in *The Savage Mind,* there is an element of enlightenment in myth, just as there is a dose of mythology in science. There is a sense in which science stripped the world of its enchanted aura only to adopt it for itself.

What happened was not that science gradually exposed the fallacies of myth and religion. To think so is in any case to write history purely at the level of ideas. It is also to ascribe religion more influence than it has taken in isolation, which is one way in which Ditchkins shares common ground with radical Islam. What took place, so Taylor argues, was a shift in the whole "social imaginary" of the early-modern epoch, one involving changes in the perception of time, space, sovereignty, the self, society, the body, discipline, and the like, of which scientific rationality was simply one element. It is not that myth gave way to fact, but that one moral outlook yielded to another. Scientific rationality represented a new form of human self-understanding, not simply a negation of what went before. It was sustained by its own ontological and symbolic framework, not just by a hard-headed rejection of such things. It is not as though an eternal, universal rationality, having patiently bided its time through long centuries of darkness, was able finally to fight its way through the rubbish dump of religious credulity under which it had been buried.

The evolution of modern, scientific rationality represents an inestimable gain. Those postmodernists who cast doubt on the value of science will presumably not be expecting a surgical operation when their hearts start to pack up, or do anything quite as dodgy as setting foot on an aircraft. But it is typical of Ditchkins's prejudice that he does not also register the losses involved in scientific rationality as we know it, in reducing reality to a stark confrontation between a bodiless subject and an inert object. If what we might risk calling postmodern science challenges this stale Cartesian dualism, it does so in ways that hark back to the premodern. Thomas Aquinas, for example, sees the encounter between subject and object not as a confrontation but as a collaboration, in which the mind actively participates in reality and, by raising the inherent intelligibility of objects to light, brings both them and its own powers to fruitful self-realization.[11] The world becomes somehow more real in the act of being understood, while the mind comes into its own in the process of doing so. Contrary to all subjective idealism, the emphasis in this reciprocity lies for Aquinas on the side of the object, as it does for Theodor Adorno. He would have had no truck with the modern or postmodern conception of a human subject projecting its arbitrary meanings on to an intrinsically meaningless world.

Whatever else one might think of the doctrine of Creation, it is at least a salve for humanist arrogance. The world for Aquinas is not our possession, to be molded and manipulated how we please, but a gift which incarnates an unknowable otherness, one whose material density and autonomy must be respected. This respect, at least, is one feature that theologians share in common with scientists. When it comes to knowledge, there is no question for Aquinas of Cartesian or empiricist "representations," "mental images," or "sense data": when we see an elephant we see an elephant, not a private mental picture or an irregular gray patch on our eyeballs. In the act of knowing, subject and object are at one. There is thus no space through which skepticism might enter. As Heidegger commented about such skepticism, what is scandalous is not the possibility that there might be nothing out there, but the act of seriously indulging this fantasy in the first place. Because Aquinas, like the Heidegger who so grievously misunderstood him, views the self as corporeal—as an active project of engagement with the world, rather than a detached, contemplative window onto it—there can be no question of postmodern skepticism. Knowledge is simply one moment or aspect of our bodily collusion in reality, a moment which modernity falsely abstracts and enshrines.

Doing, Aquinas remarks in *Contra Gentiles,* is the ultimate perfection of each thing. Being for Aquinas is an act rather than an entity. Even God is more of a verb for him than a noun. The body itself dismantles the duality between subject and object. It is how, as a participatory agent in the world, I always find myself in the midst of it, rather than peering dispassionately out at it through the arches of my eye sockets. Aquinas would no doubt have shared Wittgenstein's bemusement at the commonplace phrase "the external world." In what sense is a laburnum tree "outside" me, rather than alongside me? If I see it as "outside," then the real me must be somehow squatting inside my own body, like a man operating a crane. And who is operating him?

For Aquinas, as for Heidegger and Wittgenstein, our experience of the world is a function of our bodily engagement in it. If this experience takes a discursive rather than intuitive form, it is because the kind of material creatures we are forbids any unmediated presence to ourselves. Logocentrism is for the angels. It is true that Aquinas can avoid skepticism by invoking the Almighty, who is the ground of both being and knowing and thus the guarantee of their harmonious correspondence. Indeed, this preestablished harmony is also for Aquinas the occasion for an aesthetics. "No epistemology without theology" might be the unspoken slogan here. Yet whatever the theological basis of such a theory of knowledge, or the quaintness of supposing that a hair dryer becomes more of a hair dryer the more I know it, it is surely a richer, more dynamic, more up-to-date and generally more captivating theory than the old-fashioned rationalist model which Ditchkins seems to take for granted. It is certainly closer to Karl Marx than it is to John Locke.

The radical shift in the social imaginary which Charles Taylor records, like all such transformations, reflected a deep-seated change in social practice. It was not simply a matter of religious obscurantism fading before the unsullied light of Reason. It was also a question of different conceptions of rationality. Reason for Augustine, Anselm, and Aquinas is indissociable from certain ethical, ontological, metaphysical, and even aesthetic commitments which simply fall out of the modernist world picture. It is equally inseparable from a certain legacy of *sapientia* or wisdom. It follows that if the question "Is faith in God rational?" is posed from within a different (procedural, positivist, or verificationist) conception of reason, one for which the real is whatever can be experimentally verified or rationally deduced, it is almost bound to answer itself.[12] One need not capitulate to a view of the world as a host of mutually incommensurable rationalities to recognize that the criteria of what counts as correctness or well-foundedness in, say, anthropology are not the same as in art history. We should not assume that we know exactly what science consists in, and then see if we can fit other ways of talking (psychoanalysis, for example) into this paradigm. What if the point of psychoanalysis in this respect were to transform the paradigm itself? Jürgen Habermas's notion of communicative rationality may pass as an acceptable form of reason in Continental Europe, but its credentials are eyed much more suspiciously in Anglo-Saxon philosophy.

Science and rationality (though Taylor does not put it

this way himself) are language games bound up with what we do; and a transformation in our language games generally reflects an upheaval in material forms of life. Radical changes in representations, so Taylor insists, can make sense only against such a cultural background. We had now landed ourselves with a world of social practices in which transcendence made increasingly little sense. This, perhaps, is akin to what Marx had in mind when he inquired how epic poetry could still be produced in the age of steam power. In such conditions, certain deep questions could no longer be posed, while some groundbreaking new ones soon emerged.

A new, prestigious image of Man was born as free, controlling, agentlike, autonomous, invulnerable, dignified, self-responsible, self-possessed, contemplative, dispassionate, and disengaged. It is this historically specific, morally checkered image that Ditchkins celebrates as Reason itself. For him, it represents Man's coming of age. He does not see that this maturity, magnificently expressed in the liberalism of Immanuel Kant, is inseparable from a certain infantile anxiety. Agency, control, and autonomy are admirable virtues, but they are also attempts to master a world now felt to be threateningly alien. Sovereignty proves to be inseparable from solitude. At the peak of his assurance, Enlightenment Man finds himself frighteningly alone in the universe, with nothing to authenticate himself but himself. His dominion is accordingly shot through with a sickening sense of arbitrariness and contingency, which will grow more acute as the modern age unfolds. What is the point of extracting from the world with one hand values which the other hand has just put in? What is it for the human subject to stand on a foundation which is itself?

Transcendence, however, did not simply go away. In one sense, this is precisely what Ditchkins is complaining about; but the matter is more complex than that. The less plausibly religion seemed to answer to the human desire for a realm beyond science, material welfare, democratic politics, and economic utility, the more robustly literature, the arts, culture, the humanities, psychoanalysis, and (the most recent candidate) ecology have sought to install themselves in that vacant spot. If the arts have accrued an extraordinary significance in a modern era for which they are, practically speaking, just another kind of commodity, it is because they provide an ersatz sort of transcendence in a world from which spiritual values have been largely banished.

This, I imagine, is one reason why Christopher Hitchens is not only a crusading atheist but a professor of literature at an American university. For him and some of his friends, literature represents one of the last sanctuaries of the human spirit in a naughty world. It is a name for how even the most pious of rationalists does not live by reason alone, but by an abiding faith in a certain unfathomable creativity. I myself have been teaching literature for forty-five years, and would wager that I love the stuff as dearly as Hitchens does. I would simply point out that if we are to look to literature for our mode of transcendence, we are most certainly in deep trouble. This is not necessarily because we should look to religion instead. It is because, from Matthew Arnold and F. R. Leavis to I. A. Richards, new criticism, Northrop Frye, and George Steiner, the campaign to convert literature into a pseudo-religion has ended up doing it considerable damage. Literature is both more and less important than that.

What is peculiar to the modern age, Charles Taylor writes, in contrast with the temporally stratified premodern one, is the rise of a single "narrative of human self-realisation, variously understood as the story of Progress, or Reason and Freedom, or Civilisation or Decency or Human Rights" (716). One need hardly add that Taylor is not opposed to these ideals, as long as they are suitably lowercased. Everyone is for progress, reason, freedom, and decency, just as everyone admires Nelson Mandela. It is just Progress, Reason, Freedom, and Decency for which there are fewer takers these days. The very word "progress" is now so ideologically polluted as to be in some contexts well-nigh unusable; and it is men like Ditchkins, with their smug assurance that enlightenment would forge merrily ahead under its own steam were it not for certain residual atavisms, who have helped to discredit it with their foolishly triumphalist rhetoric. The idea of progress needs to be rescued alike from the complacency of Ditchkins and the modish skepticism of the postmodernists. There is indeed progress—as long as we bear in mind that the civilization which manifests it is also one which seems bent on destroying the planet, slaughtering the innocent, and manufacturing human inequality on an unimaginable scale.

This, strangely enough, seems to have failed to capture Ditchkins's attention. It is true that Hitchens denies that human civilization will develop "in a straight line," but only because our credulous prehistory holds us back. "We have first to transcend our prehistory," he writes in the lurid prose of a Gothic potboiler, "and escape the gnarled hands which reach out to drag us back to the catacombs and the reeking altars and the guilty pleasures of subjection and abjection" (283). Some might consider such horrors to be a touch milder than the military violence for which Hitchens himself seems to have such a relish. Rather than being dragged back to the reeking altars, we should perhaps be dragged forward to biological warfare and ecological disaster. Once we have shaken off our gullibility, Hitchens assures us, we can "consciously look forward to the further evolution of our poor brains, and to stupendous advances in medicine and life extension" (94). As long as we haven't wiped ourselves out in the meanwhile, of course. Dawkins has an equally Panglossian vision of progress. Indeed, for all his self-conscious modernity he turns out to be something of an old-fashioned Hegelian, believing in a *Zeitgeist* (his own word) involving ever-increasing moral progress, with just the occasional "reversal." "The whole wave," he rhapsodizes in the manner of some excited TV sports commentator, "keeps moving."[13] Most people in the twenty-first century, he adds, oozing moral complacency at every word, are "way ahead of our counterparts in the Middle Ages, or in the time of Abraham, or even as recently as the 1920s" (271). On this reading of history, Dawkins himself will look pretty troglodytic a century or so from now.

It is true that we have become in some ways more sensitive to the afflictions of others, as well as more self-consciously humanitarian and a lot more likely to feel some moral responsibility for strangers. These advances are greatly to be prized. But it is the grossest prejudice to list them without dwelling upon the Holocaust and two world wars. Dawkins does in fact mention the Second World War, but only to point out that the casualty rate was higher than that of the U.S. invasion of Iraq—another glowing token of our chronological ascent to saintliness. He also alludes to Hitler—a severe "reversal," he candidly confesses—but remarks that his crimes would not have been considered particularly foul in the age of Caligula or Genghis Khan.

So Hitler, too, is a symptom of moral progress. Even Goebbels might have found himself hard put to swallow that. The Führer was also born and brought up as a Catholic, as Dawkins is quick to point out, a fact which allows him to argue that this genocide at least was not the work of a fellow atheist. One had not been aware that Hitler was a particular devotee of the rosary and the Immaculate Conception. For his part, Hitchens seems to think that all forms of totalitarian thought control are religious; and though he launches a fine polemic against the Catholic church's disgusting collusion with fascism, he also tries with barefaced disingenuousness to distract attention from the fact that Nazism and Stalinism were palpably secular regimes by concentrating his fire on ecclesial support for them.

It is true, Dawkins magnanimously concedes, that Hitler slaughtered more people than Genghis did; but—so he comments as if by way of partial extenuation—he had twentieth-century technology at his disposal. Otherwise, we are invited to believe that the twentieth century, by far the bloodiest century on record, was a beacon of moral progress because one heard less racist chitchat in bars, or at least in the kind of bars Dawkins is likely to frequent. We are all getting nicer and nicer all the time. Scientific development and moral evolution would seem to go hand in hand, for Dawkins as for the dewy-eyed Victorian rationalists. The idea that science might actually have contributed to our degradation as well as to our refinement is not even cursorily considered. Nor is it by Hitchens. They are both excellent examples of finely intelligent men who have been rendered obtuse in certain respects by ideology.

There are, Dawkins is gracious enough to acknowledge, "local and temporary setbacks" to human progress (one thinks of such minor backslidings as Belsen, Hiroshima, apartheid, and so on), but the general upward trend is unmistakable. We have it, then, from the mouth of Mr. Public Science himself that aside from a few local hiccups like ecological disaster, ethnic wars, and potential nuclear catastrophe, History is perpetually on the up. Not even beaming, tambourine-banging Evangelicals are quite so pathologically bullish. What is this but an example of blind faith? What rational soul would sign up to such a secular myth?

Another such secular myth, so some scientists consider, is Dawkins's idea of "memes," cultural units which are handed down in a kind of parody of genetic transmission. In this conflation of the cultural and biological, Dawkins is a true child of nineteenth-century Positivism. It is a conflation which overlooks the fact that moral and scientific progress, far from evolving in tandem, can be in severe conflict with one another. We may have telecommunications, but we slaughter more than ever. Many a victory for civilization is potentially an advance in barbarism. Dawkins is an old-fashioned, crassly reductive system builder straight out of George Eliot's *Middlemarch,* looking for the key to all mythologies or the basic tissue of all life. All such triumphalistic totalities are fated to fail, just as *Middlemarch*'s enthusiastic totalizers are finally brought low. Such reductive systems are incompatible with the freedom which Dawkins rightly champions. In this sense, his thought is in contradiction with itself.

There is nothing wrong with a belief in the possibility of progress, as opposed to a full-blooded ideology of it. It is not inconsistent to speak up for progress while refusing to be the pawn of Progress. Ditchkins should also keep in mind the fact that many religious types have been as ardent apologists for

Progress as he is. Not all of them, however. As Alastair Crooke points out, many mainstream Islamists reject the Western narrative of inexorable progress, along with Western materialism and individualism. When a Washington think tank announced recently that "we cannot survive . . . confronted with people who do not share our values," it forgot that Western civilization managed to survive in just this way for some centuries. It was known as colonialism. What it had in mind was clearly not that Western civilization would hardly survive a full-blooded critique of its own crass materialism and selfish individualism, and might be all the better for it. Instead, the think tank concluded that the answer lay in a restoration of "Western certainties," along with a determination to use all means, including the nuclear option, against its enemies.[14]

An enlightened trust in the sovereignty of human reason can be every bit as magical as the exploits of Merlin, and a faith in our capacity for limitless self-improvement just as much a wide-eyed superstition as a faith in leprechauns. There is even a sense in which humanism, looking around our world, seems at times almost as implausible as papal infallibility. Can a world incapable of feeding so many of its inhabitants really be described as mature? Is J. L. Austin really a signal advance on Saint Augustine? As far as reason goes, what are we to make of a capitalist system which is at once eminently rational and one enormous irrationality, accumulating as it does for accumulation's sake and generating vast amounts of waste and worthlessness in the process? An excess of light, as Edmund Burke knew, can result in darkness; a surplus of reason can become (as Burke's compatriot Jonathan Swift demonstrates in *Gulliver's Travels*) a species of madness. A form of rationality which detaches itself from the life of the body and the affections will fail to shape this subjective domain from the inside, thus leaving it prey to chaos and violence. Primitivism is the flip side of rationalism.

This is one of several senses in which Enlightenment reason, inestimable though it is, can easily spawn its own opposite. The ideology of progress, for which the past is so much puerile stuff to be banished to the primeval forests of prehistory, plunders us of our historical legacies, and thus of some of our most precious resources for the future. Those who hope to sail into that future by erasing the past will simply find it returning with a vengeance. The global resurgence of religion is one example of this return of the repressed. A self-preening Enlightenment reason was largely blind to the nature of religious faith. It could not see how it encodes needs and longings which will not simply evaporate at a touch of tough-minded analysis. Because it could find in that faith nothing but laughable superstition and childish irrationality, it proved incapable of overcoming it. Ditchkins is likely to meet the same fate.

Karl Marx, who as we have seen heard in religion what he called the sigh of the oppressed creature, was rather less naïve. Religion needs to be patiently deciphered, not arrogantly repudiated. It springs from a realm to which reason should be no stranger. Only if reason is able to acknowledge the a-rational interests and desires from which it draws so much of its force can it prove sturdy enough to prevent those desires from sliding into anarchy, thus overwhelming reason itself. This is one reason why no polemic against religion pitched simply at the level of rational argument can hope to succeed.

Euripides knew all this long ago.[15] King Pentheus of *The Bacchae* is a callow rationalist whose response to the monstrously destructive, sensuously seductive Dionysus is to threaten to cut his head from his shoulders. Like the West today, he can deal with terrorism only by trying to clap it in chains. That terrorists who threaten innocent lives must be subdued by all legitimate force goes without saying. But Pentheus's resort to coercion, like much of the West's political strategy these days, is a way of disavowing the reality of what he is up against, and is thus doomed to fail as a mode of containment. For the West today, such coercion can be a way of avoiding having to examine the causes of terrorism, a project without which it can never be defeated. It is also a way of disavowing its own partial responsibility for this raging fury at its gates. An impoverished form of reason, faced with an orgy of violence, goes berserk, as one kind of excess (anarchy) provokes another (autocracy) into being. Repression, as Freudians are aware, only makes desire grow stronger.

Pentheus cannot see that reason, in order to maintain its sway, must come to terms with forces which are not reasonable in themselves. It is not that it must capitulate to them, rather strike some provisional sort of truce with them. The Theban king is therefore condemned to turn into a mirror image of the savagery he deplores. This headstrong sovereign does not see that an excessive investment in reason, of the sort we know not as reasonableness but as rationalism, can act as a defense against irrational forces within oneself. And this defense can end up provoking them. So it is that Pentheus, like Shakespeare's Angelo in *Measure for Measure,* finds himself secretly hankering for the very erotic delights he is out to censure. Rather than discerning something of his own self in this hideously brutal god Dionysus, in the act which Christianity knows as repentance, he treats this divine terrorist simply as an outlandish other to be suppressed, and so ends up being torn to pieces by the god's libidinal fury. The insanely rationalist Pentheus is unable to acknowledge this thing of darkness as his own, rather as the West is unable to confess its own part in the monstrous terror now unleashed upon it.

Ironically, the idea of progress has a religious resonance. Charles Taylor speaks of it in *A Secular Age* as a "Providence-surrogate" (279). Yet Christian eschatology is very far from the notion of some boundless evolution. The kingdom of God does not arrive as the top, triumphant note in the ascending tune of history. It is the consummation not of some stately historical evolution, but of all those flash points in history when men and women have struggled for justice, and in doing so have prefigured the advent of universal peace and justice which is the reign of God. In this way, Christian theology believes in the possibility of transforming history without the hubris of the idea of Progress. As Walter Benjamin recognized, the reign of God is simply those dispersed, often doomed fights on behalf of the oppressed seen, as it were, from the standpoint of eternity, gathered into a *nunc stans,* or singular point, where they assemble in order to be fulfilled and redeemed as a coherent narrative.[16] Modernity believes in grand narratives, while postmodernity does not; Jews and Christians hold that there is one still to come, which will operate retrospectively. As Benjamin writes: "only a redeemed mankind receives the fullness of its past."[17]

Perhaps the last word on the subject of progress should go to Theodor Adorno, victim of the triumphal historical march of the Nazis. "It would be advisable," Adorno remarks, "to think of progress in the crudest, most basic terms: that no one should go hungry anymore, that there should be no more torture, no more Auschwitz. Only then will the idea of progress be free from lies."[18]

Marxism has very little quarrel with the mighty ideals of liberal Enlightenment. It simply inquires with a certain faux naïveté why, whenever there is an attempt to realize them, they tend to twist by some inexorable logic into their opposites, so that freedom for some becomes exploitation for others, notional equality generates real inequalities, and so on. Liberalism is an exhilarating tale of emancipation from the prelates and patriarchs, insisting as it does on the scandalous truth that men and women are free, equal, self-determining agents simply by virtue of their membership of the human species. This is one of the most astonishingly radical insights ever to see the light of day, though it had a precedent in Judeo-Christianity. In its heyday, middle-class liberalism was far more of a revolutionary current than socialism has ever managed to be. Any socialism which fails to build on its magnificent achievements risks moral and material bankruptcy from the outset.

At the same time, liberalism fostered an atomistic notion of the self, a bloodlessly contractual view of human relations, a meagerly utilitarian version of ethics, a crudely instrumental idea of reason, a doctrinal suspicion of doctrine, an impoverished sense of human communality, a self-satisfied faith in progress and civility, a purblindness to the more malign aspects of human nature, and a witheringly negative view of power, the state, freedom, and tradition. Reason as a form of dominion has given birth to some of the very aspects of Western civilization to which Islamic radicalism is a pathological reaction. In this sense, the civilized and the barbarous, the enlightened and the irrational, are by no means the simple antitheses they may appear.

What was long ago named by Max Horkheimer and Theodor Adorno the dialectic of Enlightenment[19] is a form of constructive double-think that Dawkins in particular, with his sanctimonious, high-Victorian faith in scientific progress, has apparently failed to grasp. He is unquestionably right to insist on the reality of progress. Only the kind of postmodernist who ought to get out more denies that. As we have seen, however, Ditchkins, like Herbert Spencer, G. H. Lewes, and any number of Victorian ideologues, appears to believe not only in progress but in Progress—as rare and implausible a doctrine these days as a belief in the imminent return of King Arthur. Liberal rationalism, that is to say, has its own metaphysical articles of faith, and to that extent has something in common with the religious belief it excoriates. "Russell and the parsons between them have done infinite harm, infinite harm," Ludwig Wittgenstein once complained to a friend, yoking the most celebrated British antireligious liberal rationalist of his day with the very clerics against whom he inveighed.[20] How far is the dream of a thoroughly rational future a substitute for heaven? Is "Progress" the liberal-rationalist translation of "after-life"? Has liberal rationalism really got out from under religion?

A supercivilized brand of cultural supremacism, one which would no doubt find itself offended by common-or-garden racism, is now much in fashion, not least among the literary intelligentsia. Since branding others as inferior because of their race is no longer acceptable, relegating them to the outer darkness because of their religion may serve instead. The novelist Martin Amis speaks of Islamic society as "less evolved" than the West, at a time when the West is busy slaughtering hundreds of thousands of its members. It is hard to get less evolved than that. It is also dismaying, as I have noted already, to witness some Western liberals caving in to illiberalism without a struggle at the first assault on their liberal values. There is a familiar narrative behind this panic—a fable in which there is first barbarism and then civilization, but always with the possibility of barbarism returning to plague us. Civilization is dredged by sweat and toil from the fetid swamps of savagery, and is in perpetual danger of sliding back into them again. This was a familiar Victorian anxiety.

What this fable overlooks is the fact that barbarism and civilization are not only sequential but synchronic—that human civilization is among other, rather finer things a "higher" or sublimated form of violence and aggression. For radical thought, barbarism remains one of the secretly enabling conditions or barely concealed underside of that precious thing we call civilization—a barbaric subtext which with the help of George Bush and his neocon gangsters has in recent years become rather less shamefaced and subterranean. The violence which normally founds nation-states does not simply give way to a subsequent civility. Instead, it is sublimated into the business of keeping Nature aggressively under control, without which civilization finds it hard to survive. It is also sublimated into the task of defending the political state, and is now known as the military, the law, or political authority. One reason why terrorism is so alarming, quite apart from its moral obscenity, is that it reveals to civilization something of its own disavowed secret self. At the heart of freedom lurks a certain coercion, just as reason is always infiltrated by its opposite.

It would do no harm to Ditchkins's comically intemperate philippic against religion—in fact, it would mightily reinforce it—to approach the subject as the liberal rationalist he is, rather than to subject it to the kind of indiscriminate reproach which is neither liberal nor rational. Such is Richard Dawkins's unruffled impartiality that in a book of almost four hundred pages, he can scarcely bring himself to concede that a single human benefit has ever flowed from religious faith, a view which is as a priori improbable as it is empirically false. The countless millions who have devoted their lives to the selfless service of others in the name of Christ or Allah or the Buddha are simply wiped from human history—and this by a self-appointed crusader against bigotry.

As for Hitchens, *God Is Not Great* promises on page 27 to discuss "many" instances of selfless acts on the part of believers, but apart from one or two perfunctory allusions mysteriously fails to do so. We are also informed in courageously self-incriminating style that "humanism has many crimes for which to apologise" (250), but never find out exactly what they are. In any case, Hitchens's book appears to claim any good that religious men and women have achieved for the cause of secular humanism, which is rather like arguing that any advances made by feminists are due entirely to the benign influence of their fathers.

It would greatly enhance Ditchkins's moral integrity

and intellectual honesty to intersperse his mildly monomaniac diatribes on the subject of religion with the odd glancing allusion to, say, the work in alleviating human suffering which Christianity and other faiths have carried on for centuries among the wretched of the earth, or their efforts in the cause of global peace, or the readiness some religious types have shown to lay down their lives for their fellows, or those clergy who have given their lives as martyrs in the struggle against U.S.-supported autocracies. Acknowledging all this would not necessarily mean for Ditchkins sustaining a fatal wound in the ideology. Many Western liberals are careful to distinguish their criticisms of so-called radical Islam from a criticism of Islam itself; they are rarely so scrupulous when it comes to Christianity. It seems not to be the case that liberalism begins at home.

I live in Ireland, and the Irish have been shamefully abused and exploited by the Roman Catholic church in ways too familiar to recount. But the way they are doubtless least aware of is the fact that they have never been offered a version of the Gospel which it took even the slightest effort to reject. They are thus able to buy their atheism or agnosticism on the cheap. Ditchkins does just the same. And this is a form of deprivation against which one ought properly to protest, even if it is a milder form of hardship than being locked up for life by psychopathically sadistic nuns for having borne a child out of wedlock.

The Catholic church is in such understandably bad

odor in Ireland these days that people sometimes cross the street when they catch sight of a priest approaching. In the old days it was probably a landlord. Yet the cruelties and stupidities that the Irish church has perpetrated do not prevent me from recalling how, without it, generations of my own ancestors would have gone unschooled, unnursed, unconsoled, and unburied. One of my own forebears in late nineteenth-century Ireland, Dr. John Eagleton, died while still in his twenties of typhoid contracted from attending the poor. Another, Father Mark Eagleton, got into hot water with his bishop for denouncing the local landowner from the pulpit.[21] The devoutly Darwinist Dawkins, I imagine, would not take kindly to the view that acquired political characteristics can be genetically inherited, but this might seem a minor example of it.

Scarcely was the ink dry on Dawkins's *The God Delusion* and Hitchens's *God Is Not Great* than ten thousand Buddhist monks in Burma, inspired by their religious principles, marched against a brutal autocracy and were beaten, imprisoned, and murdered for their pains. It was the self-immolation of a Buddhist monk in Saigon in 1963 which first stirred American consciences over the war in Indochina. Another Vietnamese monk, Thich Nhat Hanh, became a prominent figure in the American civil rights movement and persuaded Martin Luther King to speak out against the Vietnam war. In Cambodia, where the Khmer Rouge slaughtered almost all of the country's sixty thousand monks, the monk Maha

Ghosananda became a key figure in the reconstruction of the country. In Tibet, it was Buddhist monks who in 1987 launched the first major demonstration for years, and were severely treated as a result.[22] If socialists can praise the middle classes as the most revolutionary force in history, one without which the rights and values we cherish would scarcely exist, why should Ditchkins be so curmudgeonly and intellectually shifty as to deny the magnificent achievements of religious faith, while going on to assert—a point with which one might well find oneself in agreement—that these splendid contributions to human welfare fail in the final reckoning to outweigh the horrors perpetrated by organized religion?

It is striking how avatars of liberal Enlightenment like Hitchens, Dawkins, Martin Amis, Salmon Rushdie, and Ian McEwan have much less to say about the evils of global capitalism as opposed to the evils of radical Islam. Indeed, most of them hardly mention the word "capitalism" at all, however they may protest from time to time against this or that excess of it. One has not noticed all that many of them speaking out against, say, the appalling American-backed regimes in Saudi Arabia or Pakistan. It is a familiar fact (though not, apparently, all that familiar to the U.S. media) that, thirty years to the day before the attack on the Twin Towers, the United States government violently overthrew the democratically elected government of Chile, installing in its place an odious puppet autocrat who went on to massacre far more people than died in the World Trade Center. The United States also supported for many years a regime in Indonesia that probably exterminated more people than Saddam Hussein did. Those who wrap themselves in the Stars and Stripes as a protest against Islamist atrocities should perhaps keep these facts steadily in mind.

There is good reason to believe that the outrageous violence of Islamist terrorism is among other causes a reaction to this imperial history. As Aijaz Ahmad has argued, extreme Islamists are those in whose overheated puritanical imaginations the West is nothing but a sink of corruption and debauchery, and who, having migrated into what they see as (and what often is) a hostile Western environment, "imagine for themselves a permanent, shared past that never was."[23] It is a delusion they share with many other emigrant communities, notably the American Irish. Even so, as Ahmad goes on to point out, all these potential recruits to Al Qaida stem from countries that have long, discreditable histories of European domination or colonial occupation. In the Arab world, these dissidents have seen their rulers "mortgaging their national resources to the West; squandering their rentier wealth on luxury for themselves and their ilk; and building armies that may fight each other but never the invader and the occupier." Finding no credible armies to join themselves, they proceed to fashion one of their own: secret, stateless, devoted to the propaganda of the deed. "They have seen so many countless civilians getting killed by the Americans and the Israelis," Ahmad adds, "that they do not deem their own killing of civilians as terrorism, or even comparable to what their own people have suffered. If anything, they would consider themselves *counter*-terrorists."[24]

Those who might suspect such statements of Islamist propaganda should note that their author compares the violence of such groups to that of revolutionary terrorists in tsarist Russia, while likening the "horrendously punitive and arcane regime" of the Taliban to Cambodia's Pol Pot. With an equipoise rare in such debates, however, Ahmad also reminds us that "Taliban rule was hideous but it was the only time in post-communist Afghanistan when no women were raped by the ruling elite, no rulers took bribes, no poppy was grown or heroin manufactured."[25] The relevant contrast is with the previous, U.S.-armed rule of the warlord mujahideen. If the Taliban turned the whole of the country into one vast prison for women, in conditions of mass starvation and destitution, the reign of the mujahideen meant mass orgies of rape, cesspools of corruption, and mutual annihilation.

In the past half century or so, Ahmad points out, the great majority of politically active Islamists have begun as pro-Western, and have then been driven into the anti-Western camp largely by the aggressiveness of Western policies. Among the Shia, the Khomeinist doctrine that civil government should fall under the sway of religion, and that armed insurrection was a legitimate means for achieving this end, was a stunning innovation in an Islamic tradition that had for the most part viewed political change in electoral terms. Those who sought to impose Islam through the gun constituted a very small minority. The Islamic faith forbids both suicide and the killing of civilians. What brought this violent doctrine to birth in Ahmad's view was a combination of factors. There was the suppression of the leftist and secular anti-imperialist forces in Iran by the CIA-sponsored coup of 1953, which restored the monarchy, eliminated the communists and social democrats, and created a bloodthirsty internal security force. The extreme autocracy of the Shah's regime, along with its intimate ties to the United States, were later to trigger a radical religious backlash in the shape of the Islamist revolution of 1978. With the assistance of the CIA, Iran had traveled from a nation which included secular leftists and liberal democrats to a hard-line Islamic state.

In Indonesia, a nation with the largest Muslim population in the world but also once with the largest nongoverning Communist Party as well, the secularist anticolonial government of Sukarno was overthrown in 1965 by a U.S.-supported coup, involving the single biggest bloodbath of communists in post–Second World War history, half a million or more dead, and the installation of the Suharto dictatorship. In Afghanistan, it was the United States which fostered and unleashed Islamic jihad against both native communists and the Soviets, thus laying the basis for the warlord Islamist government of the mujahideen. In Algeria, a state threatened by a democratically elected Islamist party poised to form a government called off the electoral process to loud applause from the

United States and Europe. One outcome of this suppression was to lend power to the elbow of the jihadist elements within the Islamist movement. In Egypt, the U.S.-backed regime of Mubarak repressed the parliamentary party of the Muslim Brotherhood, jailed its leaders, and rigged elections. In the subjugated Palestinian territories, the mass of the populace voted overwhelmingly for Hamas, but the election of this legitimate government triggered a Western economic stranglehold which continues to squeeze the lifeblood out of the Palestinian people.

None of this, in Ahmad's opinion or my own, provides the slightest legitimation for the use of terror. Nor is it to suggest that the West is responsible for suicide bombing. Suicide bombers are responsible for suicide bombing. It is rather to point out that the West has had an important hand in creating the conditions in which such crimes seem worth committing. Ahmad is surely right to claim that it is a "combination of domestic, anti-left and mostly autocratic right-wing (Muslim) regimes on the one hand, and, on the other, determined imperialist-Zionist policies (by the West) which is creating the objective conditions within which 'moderate,' democratic Islamism is itself giving way, in so many places, to the extremist, millenarian variety."[26] It was the West which helped radical Islam to flourish by recruiting it as a force against so-called communism—a label used to describe any country which dared to espouse economic nationalism against Western corporate capitalism. It was the West, too, which by ensuring the overthrow of those secular governments in the Muslim world that either tolerated communists or refused to align with the West (Sukarno in Indonesia, Nasser in Egypt), or which preached even a mild form of economic nationalism (Mossadegh in Iran), narrowed the space for secular politics in such societies and thus assisted the emergence of Islamist ideology.

Moreover, when Islamism grew into a powerful tendency in so many of these countries, the West handed them their "anti-imperialist" credentials on a plate by sponsoring autocratic leaders like Mubarak and the dictatorial Saudi dynasty against them, while organizing holy war against Soviet rule in Afghanistan. Meanwhile, Israel continued to flout international law in its occupation of Palestine. Islamist insurrectionists are for the most part rabidly bigoted anti-Semites, thoroughly ignorant of their own religious faith, monstrously repressive and medievalist, and ready to murder without the faintest qualm. All the same, it is hardly surprising that, as Ahmad remarks, "Islamicists just don't believe that Western law . . . will ever give them justice."[27] When Dickens's Artful Dodger, dragged into the dock at the Old Bailey, loudly protests that "this ain't the shop for justice," he is engaging in a self-pitying piece of grandstanding. He is also, as the novel perceives, perfectly correct.

Between about 1945 and 1965, Ahmad argues, most Muslim-majority societies, from Indonesia to Algeria, were extraordinarily hospitable to leftist, secular ideas. Any number of Muslim scholars, as we have noted already, have held that

Islam and socialism (or even Marxism) are mutually compatible, and have doubted the Islamic basis of private property. In the 1950s, the most massive political organization in Iraq was the Communist Party. Between the mid-1960s and late 1970s, by contrast, in the wake of the coup in Indonesia, the destruction of Arab armies in the Arab-Israeli war, and the first stirrings of Afghan jihad, leftism and secularity in the Islamic world were pitched into severe crisis, as the competing fundamentalisms of Iran and Saudi Arabia grew increasingly powerful.

Nasserism, once the dominant secular-nationalist, authoritarian-socialist current in the Arab world, was effectively destroyed by the Western-backed 1967 Israeli victory over Egypt. The Islamism that arose in the wake of that defeat arraigned Nasser for his failure to lead the Arab forces to victory over Israel. The political balance within the Arab world shifted accordingly, away from a discredited Nasserism to the monarchical, pro-Western Wahhabi fundamentalists of Saudi Arabia. What a secular politics could apparently not accomplish, a fanatically religious one would achieve instead.

The West had thus helped to lay down the conditions that would unleash future assaults on its own power. After the Israeli massacres in Jordan in 1971, Islamist ideology among the Palestinians went from strength to strength. By 1990, with the advent of an Islamist state in Afghanistan under U.S. tutelage, the resurgence of radical Islam was well under way. The world was now witness to a rabid form of religious fundamentalism—one which either made its peace with and was nurtured by the imperial West, as in Saudi Arabia, or continued the anti-imperialist struggle while establishing (or seeking to establish) theocratic, repressive, xenophobic, brutally patriarchal regimes at home. It is this militancy in which commentators like Martin Amis and many others in the West can see nothing but the actions of psychopaths, in woeful or willful ignorance of what Ahmad calls the "malignant contexts within which all sorts of cancerous growths become possible." "The secular world," he comments, "has to have enough justice in it for one not to have to constantly invoke God's justice against the injustices of the profane."[28] The solution to religious terror is secular justice.

None of this is to claim that there would be no fanatical Islamists without Western imperialism. There would indeed be, just as there would doubtless be fanatical Christian Evangelicals. It is rather that, without the vast concentration camp known as the Gaza Strip, it is not at all out of the question that the Twin Towers would still be standing. Those who resent the ascription of even this much rationality to an Islamic radicalism which they prefer to see simply as psychotic, should have a word with those in the British secret service whose task it was some years ago to monitor the Irish Republican Army. These professional antiterrorists knew well enough not to swallow a lot of cretinous tabloid hysteria about terrorists as monsters and mad beasts. They were well aware that the IRA's behavior, however sometimes murderous, was in a narrow sense of the word rational and that, without acknowledging this fact, they would be unlikely to defeat them. The CIA, with its record of kidnapping, torturing, and murdering, its support for death squads and suborning of democracy, can certainly be said to qualify as a terrorist organization; yet this does not mean that its agents are irrational. Far from it. The other side of pathologizing one's enemy is exculpating oneself. As long as we see faith as the polar opposite of reason, we shall continue to commit these errors. It is to this topic that we can now turn.

CHAPTER THREE

# Faith and Reason

Freudians and political radicals, along with a great many people who would see themselves as neither, are aware that without reason we are sunk, but that reason, even so, is not in the end what is most fundamental about us. Richard Dawkins claims with grandiloquent folly that religious faith dispenses with reason altogether, which wasn't true even of the dim-witted authoritarian clerics who knocked me around at grammar school. Without reason, we perish; but reason does not go all the way down. It is not wall to wall. Even Richard Dawkins lives more by faith than by reason. There are even those uncharitable observers who have detected the mildest whiff of obsessive irrationalism in his zealous campaign for secular rationality. His antireligious zeal makes the Grand Inquisitor look like a soggy liberal.

Indeed, Dawkins seems to nurture a positively Mao-like faith in faith itself—in the hopelessly idealist conception, for example, that religious ideology (as opposed, say, to material conditions or political injustice) is what fundamentally drives radical Islam. By contrast, Robert Pape's well-researched study of the subject, based on every suicide bombing since 1980, casts considerable doubt on this assumption.[1] In this inflation of the role of religion, Dawkins is close to many radical Islamists themselves. His belief in the power of religion is every bit as robust as the pope's.

To claim that reason does not go all thc way down, yet not thereby to cave in to irrationalism, is as hard for the political radical as it is for the Freudian or theologian. Yet it is only if reason can draw upon energies and resources deeper, more tenacious, and less fragile than itself that it is capable of prevailing, a truth which liberal rationalism for the most part disastrously overlooks. And this brings us to the question of faith and reason, which is far from simply a theological question. There is probably no greater evidence of Ditchkins's theological illiteracy than the fact that he appears to subscribe to what one might call the Yeti view of belief in God. I mean by this the view that God is the sort of entity for which, like the Yeti, the Loch Ness monster, or the lost city of Atlantis, the evidence we have so far is radically ambiguous, not to say downright dubious; and because we cannot thus demonstrate God's existence in the reasonably straightforward way we can demonstrate the existence of necrophilia or Michael Jackson, we have to put up instead with something less than certainty, known as faith.

One scarcely needs to point out even to first-year theology students what a travesty of Christian faith this is. On the most elementary questions of the theology on which he chooses to pronounce with such portentously self-regarding authority, Ditchkins is hopelessly at sea. For one thing, God differs from UFOs or the Yeti in not being even a possible object of cognition. In this sense he is more like the tooth fairy than Big Foot. For another thing, religious faith is not in the first place a matter of subscribing to the proposition that a Supreme Being exists, which is where almost all atheism and agnosticism goes awry. God does not "exist" as an entity in the world. Atheist and believer can at least concur on that. Moreover, faith is for the most part performative rather than propositional. Christians certainly believe that there is a God. But this is not what the credal statement "I believe in God" means. It resembles an utterance like "I have faith in you" more than it does a statement like "I have a steadfast conviction that some goblins are gay." Abraham had faith in God, but it is doubtful that it could even have occurred to him that he did not exist. The devils are traditionally said to believe that God exists, but they do not believe in him.

The Yeti theorists make another mistake as well. For

Christianity, faith is traditionally regarded as a question of certainty, not of plausibility, intelligent guesswork, or speculation. This is not to say that it is not also regarded as inferior to knowledge. But only fully paid-up rationalists think that nothing is certain but indisputable knowledge, if indeed such an entity exists. Faith, as the author of the *Epistle to the Hebrews* observes, is the assurance of things hoped for, the conviction of things unseen. The virtue of hope for Christianity equally involves a kind of certainty: it is a matter of an assured trust, not of keeping one's fingers crossed. Whatever else may divide science and religion, it is not for the theologian the issue of certainty. The certainty appropriate to faith is not, to be sure, of the same kind as that of a well-entrenched scientific observation like, "It's just turned red," or "The mouse is clearly drunk and the experiment is accordingly being abandoned," but neither for that matter are statements like, "I love you," or "Liberal democracy is a lot better than slavery," or "The overweening Emma Woodhouse finally gets her well-deserved comeuppance."

The relations between knowledge and belief are notably complex. A belief, for example, can be rational but not true. It was rational, given their assumptions and stock of knowledge, for our ancestors to hold certain doctrines which later turned out to be false. They thought that the sun circled the earth because it looks as though it does. (Though as Wittgenstein mischievously inquired, what would it look like if the earth turned on its axis?) Claims about the world can also be true but not in a sense rational. No doubt much of what the nuclear physicists tell us is true, but it would hardly have seemed rational to Samuel Johnson or Bertrand Russell, and stretches our own sense of the nature of things to breaking point. "Reasonable" is not quite the word that leaps spontaneously to mind when we are told that the same nuclear particle can pass through two different apertures at the same time.

It is important to recognize that just as one can have faith but not knowledge, so the opposite is also true. If God, enraged at the flourishing of atheism almost everywhere but in his own specially favored United States, were tomorrow to emblazon the words "I'M UP HERE, YOU IDIOTS!" in mile-high letters in the sky, it would not necessarily make any difference to the question of faith. Instead, it might be a bit like the aliens in the Arthur C. Clarke novel who turn up for all to behold, but who make scarcely any difference to anything and are in the end more or less ignored. For such a dramatic self-disclosure to be relevant to faith, rather than just adding an extra item to our stock of knowledge, it would have to show up in a radical transformation of what we say and do. And whether seeing such a sign would really produce such a transformation is a point that the Jesus of the New Testament angrily takes leave to doubt. Those who demand a theorem or proposition rather than an executed body are not on the whole likely to have faith in any very interesting sense of the term.

One might well imagine that if God had suddenly

appeared to the novelist Thomas Hardy over the cow shed, Hardy would not have been unduly impressed. For Hardy saw God as the fictional point at which all purely human perspectives converged; and even if some Being could occupy this location in principle, he did not see as a good evolutionary thinker how he could be relevant to a human existence which is inherently partial and perspectival. This, incidentally, is a far more original use of evolution to discredit the idea of God than any Dawkins comes up with. For Hardy, God would have nothing very interesting to say even if he existed. In one of his poems, God did indeed create the world, but has long since ceased to take an interest in it. To adapt a phrase of Wittgenstein's: If God could speak, we would not care about what he said.

Slavoj Žižek remarks in his *In Defence of Lost Causes* that fundamentalism confuses faith with knowledge. The fundamentalist is like the kind of neurotic who can't trust that he is loved, but in infantile spirit demands some irrefragable proof of the fact. He is not really a *believer* at all. Fundamentalists are faithless. They are, in fact, the mirror image of skeptics. In a world of extreme uncertainty, only copper-bottomed, incontrovertible truths promulgated by God himself can be trusted. "For [religious fundamentalists]," Žižek writes, "religious statements and scientific statements belong to the same modality of positive knowledge . . . the occurrence of the term 'science' in the very name of some of the fundamentalist sects

(Christian Science, Scientology) is not just an obscene joke, but signals this reduction of belief to positive knowledge."[2]

This is just what Ditchkins thinks as well. For him, too, religious statements are the same kind of thing as scientific ones; it is just that they are worthless and empty. Herbert McCabe, who holds the orthodox view that Christian faith is reasonable but not provable, points out that demanding watertight proofs can actually be a reactionary move. "It is a romantic myth," he writes, "that there is some kind of moral superiority about people who refuse to make up their minds because the evidence is not 100 per cent compelling. We have seen too many people who have insisted that we can't be absolutely *sure* that the Jews were persecuted in Germany, that apartheid was hideously unjust, that Catholics are persecuted in some places, that prisoners are tortured in others, and so on."[3] Besides, the scientific rationalist passes too quickly over the thorny issue of what is to *count* as certainty, as well as of the diverse species of certainty by which we live.

Nobody has ever clapped eyes on the unconscious. Yet many people believe in its existence, on the grounds that it makes excellent sense of their experience in the world. (One doubts that this includes Ditchkins, since the English tend to have common sense rather than an unconscious.) Moreover, a great deal of what we believe we do not know firsthand; instead, we have faith in the knowledge of specialists. It is also true that plenty of people believe in things that do not exist, such as a wholly just society. The whole question of faith and knowledge, in short, is a good deal more complex than the rationalist suspects.

None of this is to suggest, as Dawkins seems to suspect, that religious claims require no evidence to back them up, or that they merely express "poetic" or subjective truths. If Jesus's body is mingled with the dust of Palestine, Christian faith is in vain. We might clarify the relations between faith and knowledge here with an analogy. If I am in love with you, I must be prepared to explain what it is about you I find so lovable, otherwise the word "love" here has no more meaning than a grunt. I must supply reasons for my affection. But I am also bound to acknowledge that someone else might wholeheartedly endorse my reasons yet not be in love with you at all. The evidence by itself will not decide the issue. At some point along the line, a particular way of seeing the evidence emerges, one which involves a peculiar kind of personal engagement with it; and none of this is reducible to the facts themselves, in the sense of being ineluctably motivated by a bare account of them. Seeing something as a duck rather than as a rabbit, or as the crime of clitoridectomy rather than as a charming ethnic custom, is not a viewpoint that can be read off from the appearances. (We might note, by the way, the difference between this and the dubious notion that reason can take us so far, after which an existential leap into the dark proves essential.) You can know all there is to know as a Germanist about the *Sonnets to Orpheus,* but this is no guarantee that they will not leave you cold.

None of this should strike a scientist like Dawkins as unfamiliar. I take it that scientists are in an important sense both believers and aestheticians. All communication involves faith; indeed, some linguisticians hold that the potential obstacles to acts of verbal understanding are so many and diverse that it is a minor miracle that they take place at all. And since reason is essentially dialogical, it, too, is a matter of communication, and thus involves a kind of faith. There is no point in simply brandishing the evidence unless you have a degree of trust in those who have gathered it, have some criteria of what counts as reliable evidence, and have argued the toss over it with those in the know.

The left-wing atheist Alain Badiou, who as perhaps the greatest living French philosopher is predictably almost unknown to British academia, understands this far better than his Anglo-Saxon liberal-rationalist counterparts. Badiou grasps the point that the kind of truth involved in acts of faith is neither independent of propositional truth nor reducible to it.[4] Faith for him consists in a tenacious loyalty to what he calls an "event"—an utterly original happening which is out of joint with the smooth flow of history, and which is unnameable and ungraspable within the context in which it occurs. Truth is what cuts against the grain of the world, breaking with an older dispensation and founding a radically new reality. Such momentous "truth events" come in various shapes and sizes, all the way from the resurrection of Jesus (in which Badiou does not believe for a moment) to the French Revolution, the moment of Cubism, Cantor's set theory, Schoenberg's atonal composition, the Chinese cultural revolution, and the militant politics of 1968.

For Badiou, one becomes an authentic human subject, as opposed to a mere anonymous member of the biological species, through one's passionate allegiance to such a revelation. There is no truth event without the decisive act of a subject (only a subject can affirm that a truth event has actually taken place), which is not to say that such events are merely subjective. But there is also no subject other than one brought to birth by its fidelity to this disclosure. Truths and subjects are born at a stroke. What provokes a subject into existence for Badiou is an exceptional, utterly particular truth, which calls forth an act of commitment in which the subject is born. One thinks of the English word "troth," meaning both faith and truth. But truth is also a question of solidarity, involving as it usually does the birth of a believing community such as the church. This commitment opens up a new order of truth, and being faithful to this truth is what Badiou means by the ethical. Like divine grace, a truth event represents an invitation which is available to everyone. Before the truth, we are all equal.

Such truth events for Badiou are real enough—indeed, more real than the shabby set of illusions which commonly pass for reality. Yet they are not real in the sense that they do not "belong" to the situations from which they emerge, and cannot be counted up alongside other elements of that context. The resurrection for Christians is not just a metaphor. It is real enough, but not in the sense that you could have taken a photograph of it had you been lurking around Jesus's tomb armed with a Kodak. Meanings and values are also real, but you cannot photograph them either. They are real in the same sense that a poem is real. Like singularities in space, or mathematical sets which belong purely to themselves, Badiou-type events are a kind of impossibility when measured by our usual yardsticks of normality. Yet for all that his ideas are likely to strike the Ditchkinses of this world as Parisian gobbledygook, Badiou regards himself as an Enlightenment thinker, mustering the resources of science, equality, and universality to combat what he calls "the infamy of superstition."

I have had occasion to be critical of Badiou's ideas elsewhere.[5] There are an alarming number of problems with this theory. Badiou does, however, grasp the vital point that faith articulates a loving commitment before it counts as a description of the way things are. That it also involves an account of the way things are is clear enough, just as moral imperatives do. There is no point in issuing edicts against stealing if private property has been abolished. Anti-immigration laws are not needed at the North Pole. It is just that faith cannot be reduced to the endorsement of certain propositions which cannot be proved. What moves people to have faith in, say, the possibility of a nonracist society is a set of commitments, not in the first place a set of propositions. They must already have some allegiance to an idea of justice, and to the possibility of its realization, if they are to be stirred to action by the knowledge that men and women are being refused employment because of their skin color. The knowledge in itself is not enough to do it.

"A believer, after all, is someone in love," observes Kierkegaard in *The Sickness unto Death,* a claim that by no means applies only to religious believers. For Saint Anselm, reason is itself rooted in God, so that one can attain it fully only through faith. This is part of what he means by his celebrated assertion "I believe in order to understand"—a proposition which in a different sense could also apply to believers like socialists and feminists. Because you already take a passionate interest in women's liberation, you can come to understand the workings of patriarchy better. Otherwise you might not bother. All reasoning is conducted within the ambit of some sort of faith, attraction, inclination, orientation, predisposition, or prior commitment. As Pascal writes, the saints maintain that we must love things before we can know them, presumably because only through our attraction to them can we come to know them fully.[6] For Augustine and Aquinas, love is the precondition of truth: we seek truth because our material bodies manifest a built-in, ineradicable desire for it, a desire which is an expression of our longing for God. Aquinas's well-known demonstrations of the existence of God from reasoning about the universe already assume belief in him. Their intention is not to demonstrate God's existence as one might demonstrate the presence of a previously undetected planet, but to show believers how their faith can make sense in terms of the natural world.

Faith for Christian orthodoxy, then, is what makes true knowledge possible, which is true to some extent of everyday life as well. There is a remote parallel between this and Vladimir Lenin's claim that revolutionary theory can come to completion only on the basis of a mass revolutionary movement. Knowledge is gleaned through active engagement, and active engagement implies faith. Belief motivates action, to be sure; but there is also a sense in which you define your beliefs through what you do. Moreover, because we have come to see knowledge primarily on the model of knowing things rather than persons, we fail to notice another way in which faith and knowledge are interwoven. It is only by having faith in someone that we can take the risk of disclosing ourselves to him or her fully, thus making true knowledge of ourselves possible. Intelligibility is here closely bound up with availability, which is a moral notion. This is one of several senses in which knowledge and virtue go together. As the Duke rebukes the slanderous Lucio in *Measure for Measure:* "Love talks with better knowledge, and knowledge with dearer love" (act 3, scene 2).

In the end, only love (of which faith is a particular form) can achieve the well-nigh impossible goal of seeing a situation as it really is, shorn of both the brittle enchantments of romance and the disheveled fantasies of desire. Clinical, cold-eyed realism of this kind demands all manner of virtues—openness to being wrong, selflessness, humility, generosity of spirit, hard labor, tenacity, a readiness to collaborate, conscientious judgment, and the like; and for Aquinas, all virtues have their source in love. Love is the ultimate form of soberly disenchanted realism, which is why it is the twin of truth. The two also have in common the fact that they are both usually unpleasant. Radicals tend to suspect that the truth is generally a lot less palatable than those in power would have us believe, and we have seen already just where love is likely to land you for the New Testament. In one sense of the word, dispassionateness would spell the death of knowledge, though not in another sense. Without some kind of desire or attraction we would not be roused to the labor of knowledge in the first place; but to know truly, we must also seek to surmount the snares and ruses of desire as best we can. We must try not to disfigure what we strive to know through fantasy, or reduce the object of knowledge to a narcissistic image of ourselves.

There are those nowadays who would regard faith in socialism as even more eccentric than the exotic conviction that the Blessed Virgin Mary was assumed body and soul into heaven. Why, then, do some of us still cling to this political faith, in the teeth of what many would regard as reason and solid evidence? Not only, I think, because socialism is such an extraordinarily good idea that it has proved exceedingly hard to discredit, and this despite its own most strenuous efforts. It is also because one cannot accept that this—the world we see groaning in agony around us—is the only way things could be, though empirically speaking this might certainly prove to be the case; because one gazes with wondering bemusement on those hard-headed types for whom all this, given a reformist tweak or two, is as good as it gets; because to back down from this vision would be to betray what one feels are the most precious powers and capacities of human beings; because however hard one tries, one simply cannot shake off the primitive conviction that *this is not how it is supposed to be,* however much we are conscious that this seeing the world in the light of Judgment Day, as Walter Benjamin might put it, is folly to the financiers and a stumbling block to stockbrokers; because there is something in this vision which calls to the depths of one's being and evokes a passionate assent there; because not to feel this would not to be oneself; because one is too much in love with this vision of humankind to back down, walk away, or take no for an answer.

None of this runs counter to reason—as it would, say, if the world was already a nuclear waste land, or if socialism had actually been established already and we had simply not noticed. It is just that it is a different kind of thing from a scientific observation or an everyday piece of cognition—as, indeed, Ditchkins's belief in the value of individual freedom differs from such things. Ditchkins cannot ground such beliefs scientifically, and there is absolutely no reason why he should. Which is not to suggest, of course, that he is dispensed from adducing evidence for them. We hold plenty of beliefs that have no unimpeachable justification, but which are nevertheless reasonable to entertain. In fact, anti-foundationalists would claim that none of our beliefs or knowledge claims can be unimpeachably justified. If proof means whatever compels assent, it is in drastically short supply. Thomas Aquinas certainly did not believe that the existence of God was self-evident.

Yet this, needless to say, is not to suggest that the whole of our knowledge and belief is a fiction. A hunger for absolute justification is a neurosis, not a tenacity to be admired. It is like checking every five minutes that there is no nest of hissing cobras under your bed, or like the man in Wittgenstein's *Philosophical Investigations* who buys a second copy of the daily newspaper to assure himself that what the first copy said was true. Justifications must come to an end somewhere; and where they generally come to an end is in some kind of faith.

Christopher Hitchens would appear to disagree about this question of grounding. "Our belief is not a belief," he writes of atheists like himself in *God Is Not Great.* "Our principles are not a faith."[7] So liberal humanism of the Ditchkins variety is not a belief. It involves, for example, no trust in men and women's rationality or desire for freedom, no conviction of the evils of tyranny and oppression, no passionate faith that men and women are at their best when not laboring under myth and superstition. Hitchens is clear that secular liberals like himself (we lay charitably aside here his neoconservative fellow-traveling) do not rely "solely upon science and reason," so he is not contrasting belief with scientifically based propositions. What he is really doing is contrasting his own beliefs with other people's. "We [secular liberals] distrust anything that contradicts science or outrages reason," he observes (5). Most Christians do not in fact hold that their faith contradicts science—though it would be plausible to claim that in some sense science contradicts itself all the time, and that this is known as scientific progress. Hitchens fails to distinguish between reasonable beliefs and unreasonable ones. His belief that one should distrust anything that outrages reason is one example of a reasonable belief, while his belief that all belief is blind is an example of an unreasonable one.

Ditchkins does not exactly fall over himself to point out how many major scientific hypotheses confidently cobbled together by our ancestors have crumbled to dust, and how probable it is that the same fate will befall many of the most cherished scientific doctrines of the present. As for outrages to reason, there are those who would consider Hitchens's raucous support for the U.S. invasion of Iraq to be precisely that. (Dawkins, to his credit, strongly opposed the war.) Strangely, when it comes to that invasion, this garrulous columnist, well accustomed to broadcasting his opinions on everything from Mother Teresa to the café life of Tehran, is suddenly afflicted by a bout of coyness. "I am not going to elaborate a position on the overthrow of Saddam Hussein in April 2003" (25), he tells us. Why on earth not? He does, for all that, discuss the war a little, diplomatically passing over such matters as U.S. atrocities or the West's unslakable thirst for oil.

Hitchens did not, he informs us, hold his former Marxist opinions "as a matter of faith" (151), leaving us wondering whether he believed at the time that injustice could be scientifically established. Even the most positivistic of Marxists might blench at the thought. (Though he is no longer a Marxist, he feels, so he tells us, "no less radical" than he did then [153], a view of himself shared by rather fewer people than suspect Kate Winslet of being the Anti-Christ.) Later on he refers disparagingly to "people of faith" (230), apparently unaware that as a champion of both free speech and imperial aggression, neither of which can be demonstrated in the laboratory to be unequivocal goods, he must logically fall under this description himself. He lands himself in this mildly comic intellectual mess because he seems to assume that all faith is blind faith. One wonders whether this applies to having faith in one's friends or children. A lot of people do indeed have a blind faith in their own children. But this is a mistake. One cannot rule out in advance the possibility that one's fourteen-year-old son is a serial killer. One should be in principle open to this possibility, assess the evidence if called upon to do so, and, if the case seems to be watertight, cease to have faith in him. The sheer fact that he is your son makes no difference to this. All serial killers are somebody's sons.

Humanists differ from religious believers, *God Is Not Great* informs us, because they have no "unalterable system of belief" (250). One takes it, then, that Hitchens stands ready at any moment to jettison his belief in human liberty, along with his distaste for political tyrants and Islamic suicide bombers. In fact, of course, he turns out to be a skeptic when it comes to other people's dogmas and a true believer when it comes to his own. There is, by the way, nothing wrong with dogma, which simply means "things taught." The liberal principles of freedom and tolerance are dogmas, and are none the worse for that. It is simply a liberal paradox that there must be something closed-minded about open-mindedness and something inflexible about tolerance. Liberalism cannot afford to be overliberal when it comes to its own founding principles, which is one reason why the West is caught between treating its illiberal enemies justly and crushing their testicles. As British prime minister Tony Blair remarked in a classic piece of self-deconstruction: "Our tolerance is part of what makes Britain Britain. So conform to it, or don't come here." Hitchens dislikes people who "*know* they are right" (282), but most of the time he sounds very much like one of them himself. It is sheer bad faith for him to claim that he is provisional about his own liberal-humanist values. He is nothing of the kind, and there is no earthly reason why he should be. Besides, if he dislikes know-alls, how come he hangs around with some of that fundamentalist crew known as neocons?

I have been examining among other things some of the ways in which the faculty of reason does not go all the way down.

We need, for example, a commitment to reason itself, which is not itself reducible to reason. We can always ask ourselves, why discovering the truth should be considered so desirable in the first place. Certainly Nietzsche did not think so, while Henrik Ibsen and Joseph Conrad both had their doubts about it. What rancor, malice, anxiety, or urge to dominion, Nietzsche might inquire, lurks behind this obdurate will to truth? "There is no more factual basis for the claim that we have a moral duty to discover and share the truth," writes Dan Hind, "than there is for the claim that Jesus was the son of God."[8] If we are to defend reason, we must be inspired by more than reason to do so. It was not self-evident to Sorel or Schopenhauer that reason was to be prized.

There are legitimate disputes over the nature and status of rationality itself, which are far from involving a surrender to irrationalism—to what extent, for example, reason encompasses the aesthetic, imaginative, intuitive, sensuous, and affective; in what sense it might be a dialogical affair; what counts as a rational foundation; whether reason inherently implicates the values of freedom, autonomy, and self-determination; and whether it is substantive or procedural, axiomatic or contestable, instrumental or autotelic. We may ask to what extent it represents in its totalizing, all-explanatory nature a recycled version of the mythologies it sought historically to oust; whether it is to be modeled primarily on our knowledge of objects or on our knowledge of persons; and what relations the rational ego maintains with the superego and the primary processes. We may further inquire what we are to make of the fact that even before we have started to reason properly, the world is in principle intelligible in the first place; whether it is true that we reason as we do because of what we do, and whether reason is to be associated with common sense and moderation, as it is by liberal rationalists like Ditchkins, or with revolution, as it was by John Milton and the Jacobins. There are questions about whether reason only takes flight at dusk; whether it is to be contrasted with our animality or seen as an integral part of it, and so on.

For Aquinas, to quote Denys Turner, "rationality is the form of our animality . . . bodiliness is the stuff of our intellectual being."[9] Theology is in this sense a species of materialism. We reason as we do because of the kind of material creatures we are. We are reasonable *because* we are animals, not despite being so. If an angel could speak, we would not be able to understand what he said. It is hard to feel that such considerations lie to the forefront of the mind of Richard Dawkins, whose rationalist complacency is of just the sort Jonathan Swift so magnificently savaged. It is equally hard to feel that they have been much brooded upon by Christopher Hitchens, who as a superb journalist but an indifferent theorist is more at home with the politics of Zimbabwe than with abstract ideas.

In Robert Bolt's play *A Man for All Seasons,* Thomas More advances a very Catholic defense of reason, declaring that man has been created by God to serve him "in the wit and tangle of his mind." When a new version of the oath of allegiance to the king is produced, More eagerly asks his daughter what the exact wording is. What does it matter? she replies impatiently, taking a stand on the "spirit" or principle of the document. To which More himself replies in typically papist, semantic-materialist style: "An oath is made of words. I may be able to take it." Yet it is the same More who, when berated by his daughter for not seeing reason and submitting to the king, observes: "Well, in the end it's not a matter of reason. In the end it's a matter of love." Reasons run out in the end. But the end is a long time coming.

For the philosopher Fichte, faith (though not the religious variety) is prior to and foundational of all knowledge. For Heidegger and Wittgenstein, knowledge works within the assumptions embedded in our practical bound-upness with the world, which can never be precisely formalized or thematized. "It is our acting," Wittgenstein remarks in *On Certainty,* "that lies at the bottom of our language games."[10] Know-how precedes knowing. All our theorizing is based, however remotely, on our practical forms of life. Some postmodern thinkers conclude from this that reason is too much on the inside of a way of life to offer an effective critique of it. On their view, the terms of such a critique can only be derived from one's present way of life; yet it is precisely this way of life which the critique seeks to scrutinize. "Total" critique is thus ruled out of bounds, and along with it the possibility of deep-seated political transformation. But you do not need to be outside a situation to submit it to criticism. In any case, the distinction here between being inside and outside can be dismantled. It is a feature of creatures like ourselves that being able to distance ourselves critically from the world is part of the way we are bound up with it.

The implicit certainties or taken-for-granted truths which underpin all our more formal reasoning are as obvious in the case of science as anywhere else. Among the assumptions that science takes for granted, for example, is the postulate that only "natural" explanations are to be ruled in. This may well be a wise supposition. It certainly rules out a lot of egregious nonsense. But it is indeed a postulate, not the upshot of a demonstrable truth. If a scientist suddenly caught sight of the red-rimmed eye of Lucifer squinting balefully up at her through the microscope, or at least caught sight of it a sufficient number of times under rigorously controlled conditions, she would be bound by the conventional wisdom of science to abandon this working assumption, or to conclude that Lucifer is a natural phenomenon.

Science, then, trades on certain articles of faith like any other form of knowledge. This much, at least, the postmodern skeptics of science have going for them—though one should bear in mind that humanists have always been prejudiced against scientists, and as far as postmodernism goes have simply shifted their grounds. Whereas scientists used to be regarded as unspeakable yokels from grammar schools with dandruff on their collars who thought Rimbaud was a cinematic strongman, they have become in our own time the authoritarian custodians of absolute truth. They are peddlers of a noxious ideology known as objectivity, a notion which simply tarts up their ideological prejudices in acceptably disinterested guise. The opposite of science was once humanism; nowadays it is known as culturalism, a postmodern creed which postures as radical in the very act of striving violently to repress or eradicate Nature.

One does not need to subscribe to this travesty to note that science, like any other human affair, is indeed shot through with prejudice and partisanship, not to speak of ungrounded assumptions, unconscious biases, taken-for-granted truths, and beliefs too close to the eyeball to be objectified. Like religion, science is a culture, not just a set of procedures and hypotheses. Richard Dawkins declares that science is free of the main vice of religion, which is faith; but as Charles Taylor points out, "to hold that there are *no* assumptions in a scientist's work which aren't already based on evidence is surely a reflection of a *blind* faith, one that can't even feel the occasional tremor of doubt."[11] If the Virgin Mary were to put in an appearance at this very moment in the skies over New Haven, clutching the baby Jesus with one hand and nonchalantly distributing banknotes with the other, it would be more than the reputation of anyone laboring away in the Yale laboratories was worth to poke his or her head even fractionally out of the window.

There are, then, still a great many telescopes up which

science is churlishly reluctant to peer. Science has its high priests, sacred cows, revered scriptures, ideological exclusions, and rituals for suppressing dissent. To this extent, it is ridiculous to see it as the polar opposite of religion. There are those topics which in Foucaultian phrase are scientifically speaking "in the truth" at any given time, and those which happen for the moment not to be. I happen to know as a fact, for example, that the moon deeply affects human behavior, since as a mild species of lunatic I am always aware of when the moon is full even without looking (though I draw the line at baying or sprouting hair on my cheeks). I doubt, however, that scientists who valued their corporate grants would fall over themselves to investigate this remarkably well-evidenced phenomenon. It would be rather like a literary critic publishing a three-volume study of *Goosey Goosey Gander.*

Though Dawkins's *The God Delusion* is astonishingly tight-lipped about the cock-ups and catastrophes of science (he castigates the Inquisition, for example, but not Hiroshima), most of us are aware that, like almost any interesting human pursuit from staging a play to running the economy, science is a lot more dicey, precarious, anomalous, and serendipitous than its publicity agents would have us believe, and that many of its practitioners will go to quite extraordinary lengths to preserve a tried and trusted hypothesis. *The God Delusion,* by contrast, manages only one or two shadowy gestures to the fallibility of the enterprise to which its author has so flamboyantly pinned his faith. On the horrors that science and technology have wreaked upon humanity, he is predictably silent. Swap you the Inquisition for chemical warfare. Yet the Apocalypse, if it ever happens, is far more likely to be the upshot of technology than the work of the Almighty. In the long apocalyptic tradition of cosmic portents, fiery signs in the skies, and impending planetary doom, it was never envisaged that we might prove capable of bringing this about all by ourselves, without the slightest help from a wrathful deity. This, surely, should be a source of pride to cheerleaders for the human species like Ditchkins. Who needs an angry God to burn up the planet when as mature, self-sufficient human beings we are perfectly capable of doing the job ourselves?

None of these reservations about science should be taken as discrediting that loving, passionate, selfless, faithful, exhausting, profoundly ethical labor known as trying to get it right. In political life, it is a drudgery which can make the difference between life and death. This is one reason why one does not stumble across too many skeptics among the oppressed. Yet it is perfectly consistent with this claim to argue that all politics is ultimately faith-based. Trying to get it right is also a project with a religious history. Charles Taylor points out how the scientifically detached, disinterested subject of modernity has its origins in premodern religious asceticism, with its aloof *contemptus mundi.*[12] There is a curious sense in which knowing the world, for this theory of knowledge at least, involves a kind of refusal of it. Even so, there are those who for the sake of their own emancipation and well-being need to know how things stand with them—for whom, in short, objectivity in some sense of the term is urgently in their interests. There are also those rather more privileged souls, some of them known as postmodernists, who have no such need, and who are thus free to view objectivity as an illusion.

So science is about faith as well—which is not all it shares with theology. Rather as the churches have largely betrayed their historical mission, so, one might argue, has a good deal of science. I myself was for twenty years a Fellow of Wadham College, Oxford, an institution which in the late seventeenth century was home to the illustrious Royal Society. One of the Society's luminaries, John Wilkins, was Warden of the college and a brother-in-law of Oliver Cromwell. Unlike most of the rest of Oxford, the college was on the progressive side of the Civil War, and suffered for it. Wadham's traditionally maverick politics stretched all the way from the trade union sympathies of college Fellow Frederick Harrison and his circle of nineteenth-century English Positivists, to the Bloomsbury-style nonconformism of Warden Maurice Bowra (who admittedly scorned science) in the twentieth century. I would be glad to think that a radical English school might be appended to this list. Wadham's political dissidence had its roots in its radical scientific lineage, which prized freedom of thought and inquiry over loyalty to prelate and monarch. It is this progressive history which the postmodern skeptics of science tend to ignore, just as it is the fact that science belongs to a specific social history that the abstract rationalists too easily forget. Like religion, a good deal of science has betrayed its revolutionary origins, as the pliable tool of the transnational corporations and the military-industrial complex. But this should not induce us to forget its emancipatory history. Like liberalism, socialism, and religion, science stands under the judgment of its own finest traditions.

Some of those these days who dislike religion do so because they are suspicious of conviction as such, which is not quite what Voltaire found so offensive about it. In a pluralistic age, conviction is thought to be at odds with tolerance; whereas the truth is that conviction is part of what one is supposed to tolerate, so that the one would not exist without the other. Postmodernism is allergic to the idea of certainty, and makes a great deal of theoretical fuss over this rather modest, everyday notion. As such, it is in some ways the flip side of fundamentalism, which also makes a fuss about certainty, but in an approving kind of way. Some postmodern thought suspects that all certainty is authoritarian. It is nervous of people who sound passionately committed to what they say. In this, it represents among other things an excessive reaction to fascism and Stalinism. The totalitarian politics of the twentieth century did not only launch an assault on truth in their own time; they also helped to undermine the idea of truth for future generations. The line between holding certain noxious kinds of belief, and holding strong beliefs at all, then becomes dangerously unclear. Conviction itself is condemned as dogmatic.

Certainties may indeed destroy. But they may also liberate, a point which Jacques Derrida, with his quasi-pathological distaste for the determinate, never seemed capable of grasping. There is nothing oppressive about being certain that your wages have just been cut. For their part, liberals hold the conviction that they should tolerate other people's convictions. On the whole, they are more concerned with the fact of other people's convictions than with their content. They can even be more zealous in the cause of other people's convictions than in their own. Our age is accordingly divided between those who believe far too much and those who believe far too little—or as Milan Kundera would put it, between the angelic and the demonic.[13] Each party draws sustenance from the other. The age is equally divided between a technocratic reason which subordinates value to fact, and a fundamentalist reason which replaces fact with value.

Faith—any kind of faith—is not in the first place a matter of choice. It is more common to find oneself believing something than to make a conscious decision to do so—or at least to make such a conscious decision because you find yourself leaning that way already. This is not, needless to say, a matter of determinism. It is rather a question of being gripped by a commitment from which one finds oneself unable to walk away. It is not primarily a question of the will, at least as the modern era imagines that much fetishized faculty. Such a cult of the will characterizes the United States. The sky's the limit, never say never, you can crack it if you try, you can be anything you want: such are the delusions of the American dream. For some in the USA, the C-word is "can't." Negativity is often looked upon there as a kind of thought crime. Not since the advent of socialist realism has the world witnessed such pathological upbeatness. This Faustian belief in Man's infinite capabilities is by no means to be confused with the virtue of hope. As long as it exists, however, belief will continue to be falsely linked to so-called acts of will, in a voluntaristic misunderstanding of how we come by our convictions.

The Christian way of indicating that faith is not in the end a question of choice is the notion of grace. Like the world itself from a Christian viewpoint, faith is a gift. This means among other things that Christians are not in conscious possession of all the reasons why they believe in God. But neither is anyone in conscious possession of all the reasons why they believe in keeping fit, the supreme value of the individual, or the importance of being sincere. Only ultrarationalists imagine that they need to be. Because faith is not wholly conscious, it is uncommon to abandon it simply by taking thought. Too much else would have to be altered as well. It is not usual for a life-long conservative suddenly to become a revolutionary because a thought has struck him. This is not to say that faith is closed to evidence, as Dawkins wrongly considers, or to deny that one can come to change one's mind about one's beliefs. We may not choose our beliefs as we choose our starters; but this is not to say that we are just the helpless prisoners of them, as neopragmatists like Stanley Fish tend to imagine. Determinism is not the only alternative to voluntarism. It is just that more is involved in changing really deep-seated beliefs than just changing your mind. The rationalist tends to mistake the tenacity of faith (other people's faith, anyway) for irrational stubbornness rather than for the sign of a certain interior depth, one which encompasses reason but also transcends it. Because certain of our commitments are constitutive of who we are, we cannot alter them without what Christianity traditionally calls a conversion, which involves a lot more than just swapping one opinion for another. This is one reason why other people's faith can look like plain irrationalism, which indeed it sometimes is.

CHAPTER FOUR

# Culture and Barbarism

Why are the most unlikely people, including myself, suddenly talking about God? Who would have expected theology to rear its head once more in the technocratic twenty-first century, almost as surprisingly as some mass revival of Zoroastrianism or neo-Platonism? Why is it that my local bookshop has suddenly sprouted a section labeled "Atheism," and might even now be contemplating another one marked "Congenital Skeptic with Mild Baptist Leanings"? Why, just as we were confidently moving into a posttheological, postmetaphysical, even posthistorical era, has the God question suddenly broken out anew? Can one simply put it down to falling towers and fanatical Islamists?

I don't really think we can, at least not for the most part. Certainly Ditchkins's disdain for religion did not sprout from the ruins of the World Trade Center. It is true that some of the debate took its cue from there—an ominous fact, since intellectual debate is not at its finest when it springs from grief, hatred, hysteria, humiliation, and the urge for vengeance, along with some deep-seated racist fears and fantasies. 9/11, however, was not really about religion, any more than the thirty-year-long conflict in Northern Ireland was over papal infallibility. (It says much about Dawkins's obsession with religion that he subscribes in *The God Delusion* to the fallacy that the struggle in Northern Ireland was one over varieties of Christian belief.) Radical Islam generally understands exceedingly little about its own religious faith, and there is good evidence, as we have seen, to suggest that its actions are for the most part politically driven.

There are other reasons, too, to doubt this rather glib thesis. For one thing, Islamic fundamentalism confronts Western civilization not only with blood and fire, but with the contradiction between the West's own need to believe and its chronic incapacity to do so. The West now stands eyeball-to-eyeball with a full-blooded "metaphysical" foe for whom absolute truths and foundations pose no problem at all (would that they did!)—and this at just the point when a Western civilization in the throes of late modernity, or postmodernity if you prefer, has to skate by on believing as little as it decently can. In post-Nietzschean spirit, it appears to be busily undermining its own erstwhile metaphysical foundations with an unholy mélange of practical materialism, political pragmatism, moral and cultural relativism, and philosophical skepticism. All this, so to speak, is the price you pay for affluence.

It is not quite that, just as the West was in the act of abandoning grand narratives, a new one—that of Islamist terror—broke out to confound it. To put it that way misses the connection between the two events. It also makes the situation sound more ironic than it actually is. The much-trumpeted Death of History, meaning that capitalism is now the only game in town, reflects the arrogance of the West's project of global domination; and it is that aggressive project which has triggered a backlash in the form of radical Islam, thus disproving the thesis that history is over. In this sense, the very act of attempting to close history down has sprung it open again. It is not the first time this has happened. Assured since the fall of the Soviet bloc that it could proceed with impunity to pursue its own global interests, the West overreached itself, found itself confronting a freshly insurgent antagonist, and in doing so discredited the postmodern thesis that grand narratives were at an end. Just when ideologies in general seemed to have packed up for good, the declining global hegemony of the United States put them back on the agenda in the form of a peculiarly poisonous brand of neoconservatism. A small cabal of fanatical dogmatists occupied the White House and proceeded to execute their well-laid plans for world sovereignty, like characters in some second-rate piece of science fiction. It was almost as bizarre as Scientologists taking over 10 Downing Street, or *Da Vinci Code* buffs patrolling the corridors of the Elysée Palace.

Advanced capitalism is inherently agnostic. This makes it look particularly flaccid and out of shape when its paucity of belief runs up against an excess of the stuff—not only an external excess, but an internal one too, in the form of the various homegrown fundamentalisms. Modern market societies tend to be secular, relativist, pragmatic, and materialistic. They are this by virtue of what they do, not just of what they believe. As far as these attitudes go, they do not have much of a choice. The problem is that this cultural climate also tends to undermine the metaphysical values on which political authority in part depends. Capitalism can neither easily dispense with those metaphysical values nor take them all that seriously. As President Eisenhower once announced in Groucho Marx style: "Our government makes no sense unless it is founded on a deeply felt religious belief—and I don't care what it is."[1] Religious faith in this view is both vital and vacuous. God is ritually invoked on American political platforms, but it would not do to raise him in a committee meeting of the World Bank. It would be like appealing to the Platonic Forms or the World Spirit in choosing your wallpaper. The ideologues of the religious right, aware in their own way that the market is ousting metaphysics, then seek to put those values back in place, which is one of several senses in which postmodern relativism breeds a red-neck fundamentalism. Those who believe very little rub shoulders with those ready to believe almost anything. With the advent of Islamist terrorism, these contradictions have been dramatically sharpened. It is now more than ever necessary that the people should believe, at just the point where the Western way of life deprives them of much incentive for doing so.

Liberalism of the economic kind rides roughshod over peoples and communities, triggering in the process just the kind of violent backlash that liberalism of the social and cultural kind is least capable of handling. In this sense, too, terrorism highlights certain contradictions endemic to liberal capitalism. We have seen already that liberal pluralism cannot help involving a certain indifference to the content of belief, since liberal societies do not so much hold beliefs as believe that people should be allowed freely to hold beliefs. Such cultures display a certain creative indifference to what people actually believe, as long as those beliefs do not jeopardize these very principles of freedom and tolerance. Liberal society's *summum bonum* is to leave believers to get on with it unmolested—rather as the English would walk by if you were bleeding at the roadside, not because they are hard-hearted but because they would be loath to interfere with your privacy.

Such cultures foster a purely formal or procedural approach to belief, which involves keeping too-entrenched faiths or identities at a certain ironic arm's length. Liberal society is in this sense one long, unruly, eternally inconclusive argument, which is a source of value but also of vulnerability. A tight consensus is desirable in the face of external attack; but is harder to pull off in liberal democracies than in any other kind of state, not least when they turn multicultural. Liberal lukewarmness about belief is likely to prove a handicap at points of political crisis, especially when one finds oneself confronted with a full-bloodedly metaphysical enemy. The very pluralism to which you appeal as an index of your spiritual strength may have a debilitating effect on your political authority, not least when you are up against zealots who regard pluralism as a form of intellectual cowardice. The idea, touted in particular by some Americans, that Islamic radicals are envious of Western freedoms is about as convincing as the suggestion that they are secretly hankering to sit in cafés smoking dope and reading Gilles Deleuze.

The social devastation wreaked by economic liberalism means that some besieged groups can feel secure only by clinging to an exclusivist identity or unbending doctrine. If their forms of belief are so extreme, however, it is partly because advanced capitalism has little alternative to offer them. This is among other reasons because it seeks to win from its citizens the kind of automated, built-in consent which does not depend all that much on what they believe. Advanced capitalism is not the kind of regime that need exact too much spiritual commitment from its subjects. Zeal is more to be feared than encouraged. As long as the populace get out of bed, roll into work, consume, pay their taxes, and refrain from beating up police officers, what goes on in their heads and hearts is for much of the time a strictly secondary affair. The authority of the system is for the most part sealed in practical, material ways, not by ideological faith. Belief is not what keeps the system ticking over, as it is what keeps the Salvation Army ticking over. This, too, is an advantage in "normal" times, since demanding too much belief from men and women can easily backfire. It is much less of a benefit in times of political tumult.

The literary critic Catherine Gallagher has suggested that reading fiction is among other things an imaginative exercise in this business of sitting loose to belief.[2] Reading fiction while knowing that it is fiction, she argues, involves a degree of "ironic credulity," believing and not believing at the same time. It is interesting in this respect (though Gallagher does not touch on the fact) that one of the greatest of English novelists, Samuel Richardson, did not want his novel *Clarissa* to be thought a real-life story, but neither did he want to announce in the preface that the work was fictional. If the novel was taken to be a real narrative, its exemplary status might be undercut, and with it its moral force; if it was thought to be fiction, its moral force might be fatally weakened. All realist fiction engages in this balancing act, seeking to generalize its contents without damage to their specificity. Gallagher's point, anyway, is that readers are invited to feel superior in their worldly skepticism to the credulous innocence of the fictional hero or heroine. The story becomes a kind of speculative venture in which one does not invest too quickly, keeping one's options open and remaining alert to other possibilities. Since the reader does not trust in the reality of the characters, she can think her way around them at leisure, admiring their plausibility and the craftsmanship with which they are fabricated. "Such flexible mental states," Gallagher writes, "were the sine qua non of modern subjectivity."[3] In its ironic refusal to empathize and identify, fiction becomes a kind of alternative to ideology. Or at least, one might claim, to ideology of a certain kind—for not all ideology is free of irony and self-reflection. It is perfectly possible to confess what a terrible sexist one is.

Multiculturalism at its least impressive blandly embraces difference as such, without looking too closely into what one is differing over. It tends to imagine that there is something inherently positive about having a host of different views on the same subject. It would be interesting to know whether it considers this to be the case when it comes to asking whether the Holocaust ever took place. Such facile pluralism therefore tends to numb the habit of vigorously contesting other people's beliefs—of calling them arrant nonsense or unmitigated garbage, for example, as one must of course preserve the right to do. This is not the best training ground for taking on people whose beliefs can cave in skulls. One of the more agreeable aspects of Christopher Hitchens's polemic against religion is that he is properly unafraid to declare that he thinks it poisonous and disgusting. Perhaps he finds it mildly embarrassing in his new post-Marxist persona that "Religion is poison" was the slogan under which Mao launched his assault on the people and culture of Tibet. But he is right to stick to his guns even so. Beliefs are not to be respected just because they are beliefs. Societies in which any kind of abrasive criticism constitutes "abuse" clearly have a problem. "Abuse" is one of the latest American buzzwords, including as it does such unpardonable offenses as conducting a heated argument with someone, or recounting unpalatable political facts which another person would prefer not to hear.

A surfeit of belief is what agnostic, late-capitalist civilization itself has helped to spawn. This is not only because it has helped to create the conditions for fundamentalism. It is also because when reason becomes too dominative, calculative, and instrumental, it ends up as too shallow a soil for a reasonable kind of faith to flourish. As a result, faith lapses into the kind of irrationalism which theologians call fideism, turning its back on reason altogether. From there, it is an easy enough step to fanaticism. Rationalism and fideism are each other's mirror image. The other side of a two-dimensional reason is a faith-based reality. "Where reason has retreated," writes John Milbank, "there, it seems, faith has now rushed in, often with violent consequences."[4] If reason has trouble with value, faith has problems with fact. Neoconservatism is a species of fideism, untroubled in its ideological ardor by anything as trifling as reality. Fundamentalism is among other things the faith of those driven into zealotry by a shallow technological rationality which sets all the great spiritual questions cynically to one side, and in doing so leaves those questions open to being monopolized by bigots.

Conversely, reason, as I have argued already, has to ground itself in something other than itself to be authentic *as reason.* If it grounds itself largely in material interests and political dominion, rather than in some kind of loving fidelity or peaceable community, faith and reason will spin apart from each other, becoming those bloodless caricatures of themselves known as fideism and rationalism. There is another sense, too, in which a paucity of faith leads to a surplus of it, which is simply that if the West really did have faith in a gospel of peace, justice, and fellowship, it would presumably not spend so much of its time burning Arab children to death, and thus would not have to worry quite so much about people crashing aircraft into nuclear reactors in the name of Allah. Nor would Muslims who knew something about their religious faith consider doing so. There can surely be no doubt that if these values really were to prevail, the world would be a great deal better off. Justice would be brought to bear on the conflict between Palestine and Israel. Humanity would regard itself as exercising stewardship rather than dominion over Nature. War would give way to peace. Forgiveness would mean among other things forgiving the crippling debts which burden poor nations. Mutual responsibility would oust selfish individualism.

It is just that, for all this to happen, believers themselves would have to take their own values seriously. And there seems to be fat chance of that.

Economic liberalism has generated great tides of global migration, which within the West gives birth to so-called multiculturalism. There is a contradiction here, too, since the more capitalism flourishes on a global scale, the more it threatens in this respect to loosen the hold of the nation-state over its subjects. Culture is what beds power down, interweaving it with our lived experience and thus tightening its grip upon us. An authority which fails to do this will loom up as too abstract and aloof, and thus fail to secure its citizens' unqualified allegiance. If power is to win loyalty, it must translate itself into culture. But a power which has to bed itself down in many diverse cultures simultaneously is at a signal disadvantage. A think tank at the heart of Britain's defense and security establishment recently published a report which claimed that a "misplaced deference to multiculturalism" which fails "to lay down the line to immigrant communities" was weakening the fight against political extremists. The problem, the report warned, was largely one of social fragmentation, portraying as it did a multicultural nation increasingly divided over its history, identity, aims, and values. The nation's liberal values, in short, were undermining the liberal values it sought to protect from terrorism.

Take the argument in Britain over so-called British values, to which, so it is argued, new immigrants to the country need to be introduced. There is an insuperable problem about this project, since there are no British values. Nor are there any Serbian or Peruvian values. No nation has a monopoly on justice and humanity, fairness and compassion. It is true that some cultures cherish one kind of value more than others (Arabs and hospitality, for example, or the British and emotional self-discipline). But there is nothing inherently Arab about hospitality, or inherently British about not throwing a tantrum. Tolerance and compassion, like sadism and sexual jealousy, can be found anywhere on the planet. Nations like North Korea or Saudi Arabia flout moral values such as the freedom of the individual, while nations like Britain and the United States violate the moral injunction to welcome the stranger and care for the poor. But this is no argument against the universal nature of such values.

It was one of the mighty achievements of the radical Enlightenment to reject the idea that virtue or vice depend on your ethnic origin. Nobody is morally better off because they were born in Boston rather than Bosnia. It is true that being raised in a well-heeled environment makes certain kinds of virtue easier, as opposed to growing up in a society ridden with strife, scarcity, and sectarian hatred. But easy virtue is less meritorious, while people who manage to be generous, courageous, and forgiving in unpropitious surroundings are all the more deserving of praise. They might also have more opportunity to exercise some really resplendent virtues, an opportunity usually denied to those who live in Hatfield or the Hamptons.

Postmodernists who deny the existence of universal values in the name of cultural difference can find themselves unwittingly in cahoots with the tub thumpers for Trafalgar and the groupies of Saint George. The fundamental moral values of the average Muslim dentist who migrates to Britain are much the same as those of an English-born plumber. Neither will typically maintain that lying and cheating are the soundest policy, or that children are at their finest when regularly beaten to a pulp. They may well have different customs and beliefs; but what is striking is the vast extent of common ground between them on the question of what it is to live well. As far as religious morality goes, it is hard to slide a cigarette paper between Allah and Jehovah. This, indeed, is part of what Ditchkins finds so repugnant about it.

It is easy, then, to see why a diversity of cultures should present power with a problem. Multiculturalism poses a threat to the existing order not only because it can act as a breeding ground for terrorists, but because the political state depends on a reasonably tight cultural consensus in order to sell its materially divisive policies to its citizens. When some of those for whom culture means mostly *Mansfield Park* and *The Magic Flute* begin vigorously debating culture as language, dress, and religious custom, one can be reasonably sure that a political crisis is at hand.

British prime ministers believe in a common culture, just as New Left thinkers like Raymond Williams and E. P. Thompson did. It is just that what prime ministers mean by a common culture is that everyone should share their own beliefs so that they won't end up bombing London underground stations. The truth, however, is that no cultural belief is ever extended to sizeable groups of newcomers without being transformed in the process. It is this that some simple-minded philosophy of "integration" fails to recognize. There is no assumption in the White House, Downing Street, or the Elysée Palace that their own beliefs might be challenged or changed in the act of being extended to others. A common culture on this view is one which incorporates outsiders into an already established, unquestionable framework of values, while leaving them free to engage in whichever of their quaint customs poses no threat to this preordained harmony. Such a policy appropriates newcomers in one sense, while leaving them well alone in another. It is at once too possessive and too hands-off. A common culture in a more radical sense of the term is not one in which everyone believes the same thing, but one in which everyone has equal status in cooperatively determining a way of life in common.

If this is to include those from cultural traditions which are currently marginal, then the culture we are likely to end up with will be very different from the one we have now. For one thing, it will be more diverse. A culture which results from the active participation of all its members is likely to be more mixed and uneven than a uniform culture which admits new members only on its own terms. In this sense, equality generates difference. It is not a question of mustering a diversity of cultures under the common umbrella of Britishness, but of putting that whole received identity into the melting pot and seeing what might emerge. If the British or American way of life really were to take on board the critique of materialism, hedonism, and individualism of many devout Muslims, rather than Muslims simply to sign on for a ready-made British or American culture, Western civilization would most certainly be altered for the good. This is a rather different vision from the kind of multiculturalism which leaves Muslims and others well alone to do their own charmingly esoteric stuff, commending them from a safe distance.

Part of what has happened in our time is that God has shifted over from the side of civilization to the side of barbarism. He is no longer the short-haired, blue-blazered God of the West—or if he is, then, this image of him is now current almost only in the United States, not in Porto or Cardiff or Bologna. Instead, he is a wrathful, dark-skinned God who if he did create John Locke and John Stuart Mill, has long since forgotten the fact. One might go further and claim that the new form of barbarism is known as culture. One can still speak of the clash between civilization and barbarism; but a more subtle form of the same dispute is to speak of a conflict between civilization and culture. Civilization means universality, autonomy, prosperity, plurality, individuality, rational speculation, and ironic self-doubt; culture signifies all those unreflective loyalties and allegiances, as apparently as built into us as our liver or pancreas, in the name of which men and women are in extreme circumstances prepared to kill. Culture means the customary, collective, passionate, spontaneous, unreflective, unironic, and a-rational. It should come as no surprise, then, that we have civilization whereas they have culture. More precisely, colonizing nations are civilizations, while most colonies or former colonies are cultures.

It is true that there can be no absolute contrast between culture and civilization. This is because culture in the sense of a specific way of life is the very medium of the supposedly universal values of civilization. It is the way those values get fleshed out as forms of practical reason; and unless this comes about, civilized principles will remain too abstract to be effective. To put the point rather less loftily: the transnational corporations are entirely cultureless and unlocalized in themselves, but must pay sedulous attention to how business is traditionally transacted in Colombo or Chittagong. Multiculturalism means among other things being sensitive to cultural difference so as to promote your global interests. Yet there is also an intense antagonism between civilization and culture, which the cultural supremacists among us have increasingly mapped onto a West/East axis. They are forgetful that Western civilization is ridden with cultures from end to end. They also forget that the closed culture of Islamic radicalism does not reflect Muslim civilization as a whole.

One of the most pressing problems of our age, then, is that civilization can neither dispense with culture nor easily coexist with it. Civilization is precious but fragile; culture is raw but potent. Civilizations kill to protect their material interests, whereas cultures kill to defend their identity. The more pragmatic and materialistic civilization becomes, the more culture is summoned to fulfill the emotional and psychological needs that it cannot handle. The more, therefore, the two fall into mutual antagonism. What is meant to mediate universal values to particular times and places ends up turning aggressively against them. Culture is the repressed which returns with a vengeance. Because it is supposed to be more localized, immediate, spontaneous, and a-rational than civilization, it is the more aesthetic concept of the two. The kind of nationalism that seeks to affirm a native culture is always the most poetic kind of politics—the "invention of literary men," as someone once remarked. You would not have put the great Irish nationalist Padraic Pearse on the sanitation committee.

Religion falls on both sides of this fence simultaneously, which is part of its formidable power. As civilization, it is doctrine, institution, authority, metaphysical speculation, transcendent truth, choirs, and cathedrals. As culture, it is myth, ritual, savage irrationalism, spontaneous feeling, and the dark gods. Christianity began as a culture but then became a question of civilization. Religion in the United States is still by and large a civilizational matter, whereas in England it is largely a cultural affair, a traditional way of life more akin to high tea or clog dancing than to socialism or Darwinism, which it would be bad form to take too seriously (the highly English Dawkins is in this respect egregiously un-English). One couldn't imagine the Queen's chaplain asking you if you have been washed in the blood of the Lamb. As the Englishman remarked, it's when religion starts to interfere with your everyday life that it's time to give it up. Polls reveal that most of the English believe that religion has done more harm than good, an eminently reasonable opinion unlikely to be endorsed in Dallas.

Since culture means among other things that you can't really help believing what you believe, it becomes a substitute for rational debate. This is what the champions of civilization rightly hold against it. Just as in some traditionalist societies you can justify what you do on the grounds that it was what your ancestors did, so for some culturalists you can justify what you do because your culture does it. Cultures themselves are assumed here to be morally neutral or positive, which is true if one is thinking of Iceland, the Azande, or the maritime community, but not if one is thinking of Hell's Angels, neo-fascists or Scientologists. Aijaz Ahmad points out that culture has come in some quarters to mean that this is *how* one is because of *who* one is, a doctrine shared by biologically based forms of racism.[5] Being from Scotland or Sri Lanka isn't something you get to choose, unlike being a Jesuit or hailing from the Pabloist tendency of the Fourth International—in which case it might follow that how you behave is not something you get to choose either. If culture goes all the way down, constituting our very identities, this case looks fairly plausible. An appeal to culture thus becomes a way of absolving us to some extent from moral responsibility as well as from rational argument. Just as it is part of their way of life to dig traps for tigers, so it is part of our way of life to manufacture cruise missiles. It is one of Ditchkins's strengths that whatever else he may be, he is certainly not a culturalist. Indeed, he leans much too far in the other direction.

Postmodern thought is hostile to the idea of foundations. But this really means that it is hostile to traditional versions of them. In its own case, these traditional grounds are replaced by a new kind of foundation known as culture. Culture becomes the new absolute, bottom-line, conceptual end-stop, or transcendental signifier. It is the point at which one's spade hits rock bottom, the skin out of which one cannot leap, the horizon over which one is unable to peer. This is a strange case to launch at a point in history when Nature, a somewhat passé idea until our attention was recently drawn to the fact that it seems to be about to pack up, may be on the point of trumping human culture as a whole. Nature always has the edge over culture in the end. It is known as death.

There is a certain sacred resonance to the idea of culture.

It has, after all, sought for a couple of centuries or more to serve as a secular alternative to a failing religious faith. This is not a wholly ridiculous notion. Like religion, culture is a matter of ultimate values, intuitive certainties, hallowed traditions, assured identities, shared beliefs, symbolic action, and a sense of transcendence. It is culture, not religion, which is now for many men and women the heart of a heartless world. Indeed, there are some for whom it serves as an opium substitute as well. This is true whether one has in mind the minority idea of culture as literature and the arts, or whether one is thinking of culture as a cherished way of life. As far as the former sense of culture goes, it is worth noting that most aesthetic concepts are pieces of displaced theology. The work of art, seen as mysterious, self-dependent, and self-moving, is an image of God for an agnostic age. Yet culture is not in fact able to fill the role of an *ersatz* religion, which is one reason why the idea of culture has come under so much strain in the last couple of centuries. Works of art cannot save us. They can simply render us more sensitive to what needs to be repaired. And celebrating culture in the sense of a way of life is too parochial a version of redemption.

You can seek to reconcile culture and civilization (or as some might translate these terms, the Germans and the French) by claiming that the values of civilization, though universal, need a local habitation and a name—some sector of the globe which acts as the postal address of human civility itself. And this, of course, has been the West. The West is *a* civilization, to be sure; but it is also the very essence of the thing itself, rather as France is one nation among many yet also the very essence of the intellect. If this case seems too supremacist, it is possible to come up with what seems at first glance like a rather less chauvinistic version of it. This is associated among others with the philosopher Richard Rorty—a name, incidentally, which the *Oxford English Dictionary* defines as "rowdy," "boisterous," "coarse," "earthy," and "fun-loving," which is not exactly how I remember him. On this argument, you can acknowledge that Western civilization is indeed a "culture" in the sense of being local and contingent; but you can claim at the same time that its values are the ones to promote, just as though they were in fact universal. Certain similar arguments can be found in the work of the literary critic Stanley Fish.[6]

This means behaving as though your values have all the force of universal ones, while at the same time insulating them from any thoroughgoing critique. They are immune to such critique because you do not claim any rational foundation for them; and this is the effect of seeing yourself as just one culture among others. In a bold move, you can abandon a rational defense of your way of life for a culturalist one, even though the price of doing so is leaving it perilously ungrounded. "Culture" and "civilization" here felicitously coincide. The West is most certainly civilized; but since its civility descends to it from its contingent cultural history, there is no need to provide rational grounds for it. One thus wins oneself the best of both worlds. The idea of culture is not spurned, as the notion of barbarism has been. Instead, it is incorporated into civilization in a way that helps to quarantine it against fundamental challenge.

I have argued already that reason alone can face down a barbarous irrationalism, but that to do so it must draw upon forces and sources of faith which run deeper than itself, and which can therefore bear an unsettling resemblance to the very irrationalism one is seeking to repel. It is a situation that confronted Europe during the Second World War. Is rationalism or liberal humanism really enough to defeat fascism, a movement which draws for its force on powerfully irrational sources; or can it be vanquished only by an antagonist that cuts as deep as it does, as socialism claims to do? From a socialist point of view, liberal rationalism is too skin-deep a creed to tackle what is at stake; from a liberal viewpoint, socialism and fascism have too much disturbingly in common. One can read Thomas Mann's great novel *Doctor Faustus* as among other things an allegory of this dilemma. But the question of reason and its other is also a major theme of Mann's novel *The Magic Mountain.* In this work, life and death, affirmation and negation, *Eros* and *Thanatos,* the sacred and the obscene, are all closely interwoven; and this battle between the life instincts and the death instincts takes the shape of a conflict between Settembrini, the liberal rationalist and Enlightenment humanist, and the sinister Naphta, Jesuit, communist, and rebel against bourgeois Enlightenment.

Naphta is a full-blooded modernist in Satanic revolt against Settembrini's spirit of liberal modernity. He is an exponent of sacrifice, extremity, spiritual absolutism, religious zeal, occultism, impersonality, dogmatism, and the cult of death—in short, of everything which in Ditchkins's eyes represents the foulest face of humanity. He draws his life from the dark, archaic, blood-stained springs of culture, whereas the civilized Settembrini is a sunny-minded champion of reason, progress, liberal values, and the European mind. There is something of the same contrast between Zeitblom, the liberal-minded but ineffectual narrator of Mann's *Doctor Faustus,* and the demonic artist who stands at the book's center, Adrian Leverkühn.

There can be no doubt, then, which character in *The Magic Mountain* Ditchkins would find most congenial. The novel itself, however, is a trifle more subtle in its judgments. The Settembrini who celebrates life is actually at death's door, and his cosmopolitanism is among other things a parochial form of Eurocentrism. In Naphta's scornful view, his colleague's progressivism is itself obsolete and archaic, as the First World War during which the novel is set spells the ruin of all those high nineteenth-century hopes. It is significant in this respect that nobody in the clinic in which the novel's action takes place ever seems to be cured. Naphta may be pathologically in love with death, but Settembrini's buoyant humanism thrives on the repression of it. His cult of health and civilization is scandalized by the thought of disease and depravity, and can scarcely bear to contemplate such conditions. He cannot stomach the truth that to be human is among other things to be sick. He does not see that perversity and aberration are constitutive of the human condition, not just irrational deviations from it.

What the novel's protagonist, Hans Castorp, comes to learn is that there is a form of death-in-life which is the way of neither Naphta nor Settembrini. Instead, it is a matter of affirming the human humbly, nonhubristically, in the knowledge of its frailty and mortality. This tragic humanism embraces the disruptiveness of death, as Settembrini does not; but, unlike Naphta, it refuses to turn death into a fetish. Only by bowing to our mortality can we live fulfilledly. At the heart of Castorp's moving utopian vision of love and comradeship in the novel's great snow scene lurks the horrifying image of the tearing of a child limb from limb, a token of the blood sacrifice which underpins civilization itself. Having been granted this epiphany, Hans will henceforth refuse to let death have mastery over his thoughts. It is love, not reason, he muses, which is stronger than death, and from that alone can flow the sweetness of civilization. Reason in itself is too abstract and impersonal a force to face down death. But such love, to be authentic, must live "always in silent recognition of the blood-sacrifice." One must honor beauty, idealism, and the hunger for progress, while confessing in Marxist or Nietzschean style how much blood and wretchedness lie at their root. It does not seem on the face of it that this wisdom is one shared by the purveyors of Progress.

If culture can prove no adequate stand-in for religion, neither can it serve as a substitute for politics. The shift from modernity to postmodernity represents among other things the belief that it is culture, not politics, which holds center stage. Postmodernism is more perceptive about lifestyles than it is about material interests. Generally speaking, it is a lot better on identity than oil. As a form of culturalism, it has an ironic affinity with radical Islam, which also holds that what is ultimately at stake are beliefs and values. "For Islamists," writes Asef Bayat, "imperialism is embodied not simply in military conquest and economic control; it manifests itself first and foremost in cultural domination, established through the spread of secular ideas, immorality, foreign languages, logos, names, food and fashion . . . building an exclusive moral and ideological community was substituted for the social emancipation of the subaltern."[7] This is a thoroughly postmodern case.

I have argued elsewhere that Western postmodernism has some of its roots in the failure of revolutionary politics.[8] In a similar way, Islamic radicalism is born not only of a reaction against predatory Western politics, but also, as we have seen already, of the crushing of various forms of Muslim secularism, liberalism, nationalism, and socialism. Islamic fundamentalism is among other things a virulent response to the defeat of the Muslim left—a defeat in which the West has actively conspired. This is one of several senses in which the chickens are coming home to roost. In some quarters, the language of religion is replacing the discourse of politics. This, one might claim, is the direct opposite of Christian liberation theology, which seeks to unify the two. As Bayat points out, the champions of such theology never sought to Christianize the state, as radical Islamists seek to Islamize their societies. A similar culturalism marks the thought of the Western ideologue Samuel Huntington, whose influential study *The Clash of Civilizations* defines civilizations (Huntington is unsure exactly how many of these elusive beasts there are) primarily in cultural and religious terms.

If politics has so far failed to unite the wretched of the earth in the name of transforming their condition, we can be sure that culture will not accomplish the task in its stead. Culture, for one thing, is too much a matter of affirming what you are or have been, rather than what you might become. What, then, of religion? What we know as Christendom saw itself as a unity of culture and civilization. If religion has proved far and away the most powerful, tenacious, universal symbolic form humanity has yet to come up with, it is partly on this account. What other symbolic form has managed to forge such direct links between the most absolute and universal of truths and the everyday practices of countless millions of men and women? What other way of life has brought the most rarefied of ideas and the most palpable of human realities into such intimate relationship? Religious faith has established a hotline from personal interiority to transcendent authority—an achievement upon which the advocates of culture can only gaze with envy. Yet religion is as powerless as culture to emancipate the dispossessed. For the most part, it has not the slightest interest in doing so.

With the advent of modernity, culture and civilization were progressively riven apart. Faith was driven increasingly into the private domain, or into the realm of everyday culture, as political sovereignty passed into the hands of the secular state. Religion represented rather more belief than the liberal state could comfortably handle, hijack it though it might for its own legitimation. Along with the other two symbolic domains of art and sexuality, religion was unhooked to some extent from secular power; and the upshot of this privatization for all three symbolic forms was notably double-edged. On the one hand, they could act as precious sources of alternative value, and thus of political critique; on the other hand, their isolation from the public world caused them to become increasingly pathologized.

The prevailing global system, then, faces an unwelcome choice. Either it trusts in the virtues of its native pragmatism in the face of its enemy's absolutism, a risky enough enterprise; or it falls back on metaphysical values of its own, as Western fundamentalists would insist. Yet these values are looking increasingly tarnished and implausible. They might see God as the great Chief Executive Officer in the sky in Holland, Michigan, but it is a view unlikely to be endorsed in Münster or Manchester. Does the West need to go full-bloodedly metaphysical to save itself? And if it does, can it do so without inflicting too much damage on its liberal, secular values, thus ensuring there is still something worth protecting from its illiberal opponents?

If Marxism holds out a promise of reconciling culture and civilization, it is among other things because its founder was both a Romantic humanist and an heir of Enlightenment rationalism. Marxism is about culture and civilization together—sensuous particularity *and* universality, worker and citizen of the world, local allegiances and international solidarity, the free self-realization of flesh-and-blood individuals and a global cooperative commonwealth of them. But Marxism has suffered in our time a staggering political rebuff; and one of the places to which those radical impulses have migrated is—of all things—theology. It is in some sectors of theology nowadays that one can find some of the most informed and animated discussions of Deleuze and Badiou, Foucault and feminism, Marx and Heidegger.

This is not entirely surprising, since theology, however implausible many of its truth claims, is one of the most ambitious theoretical arenas left in an increasingly specialized world—one whose subject is nothing less than the nature and destiny of humanity itself, in relation to what it takes to be its transcendent source of life. These are not questions one can easily raise in analytic philosophy or political science. Theology's remoteness from pragmatic issues is an advantage in this respect. We find ourselves, then, in a most curious situation. In a world in which theology is increasingly part of the problem, as Ditchkins rightly considers, it is also fostering the kind of critical reflection which might contribute to some of the answers. There are lessons which the secular left can learn from religion, for all its atrocities and absurdities, and the left is not so flush with ideas that it can afford to look such a gift horse in the mouth.

Will either side listen to the other at present? Will Ditchkins read this book and experience an epiphany which puts the road to Damascus in the shade? To use no less than two theological terms by way of response: not a hope in hell. Positions are at present too entrenched to permit of such a dialogue. Mutual understanding cannot happen just anywhere, as some liberals tend to suppose. It requires its material conditions. It does not seem that they will emerge as long as the so-called war on terror continues to run its course.

The distinction between Ditchkins and those like myself comes down in the end to one between liberal humanism and tragic humanism. There are those like Ditchkins who hold that if we can only shake off a poisonous legacy of myth and superstition, we can be free. This in my own view is itself a myth, though a generous-spirited one. Tragic humanism shares liberal humanism's vision of the free flourishing of humanity; but it holds that this is possible only by confronting the very worst. The only affirmation of humanity worth having in the end is one which, like the disillusioned post-Restoration Milton, seriously wonders whether humanity is worth saving in the first place, and can see what Jonathan Swift's king of Brobdingnag has in mind when he describes the human species as an odious race of vermin. Tragic humanism, whether in its socialist, Christian, or psychoanalytic varieties, holds that only by a process of self-dispossession and radical remaking can humanity come into its own.[9] There are no guarantees that such a transfigured future will ever be born. But it might arrive a little earlier if liberal dogmatists, doctrinaire flag-wavers for Progress, and Islamophobic intellectuals did not continue to stand in its way.

# Notes

CHAPTER ONE

## The Scum of the Earth

1. With misplaced charity, I changed this headmaster's name to "Damian" in my memoir *The Gatekeeper* (London: Allen Lane/Penguin, 2001), and was rightly chided for doing so by several of his former victims. I have accordingly outed him here.
2. My memoir *The Gatekeeper* (London: Allen Lane/Penguin, 2001) could perhaps be described an anti-autobiography.
3. Hebert McCabe, *Faith Within Reason* (London: Continuum, 2007), 76.
4. Christopher Hitchens, *God Is Not Great* (London: Atlantic, 2007), 282.
5. John C. Lennox, *God's Undertaker* (Oxford: Lion, 2007), 62.
6. Rowan Williams, "How to Misunderstand Religion," lecture given at Swansea University, Wales, 13 October 2007.
7. Quoted in Lennox, *God's Undertaker*, 58.
8. John Gray, "The Atheist Delusion," *Guardian* (March 15, 2008).
9. I use the term "Judeo-Christianity" simply to indicate certain cultural and theological continuities, not as a patronizingly

"inclusive" gesture toward Jews or as conservative ideological code for the exclusion of Muslims.

10. See Charles Taylor, *Sources of the Self* (Cambridge: University of Cambridge Press, 1989), 13–16, 81–83, 211–47.
11. See my *An Essay on Evil* (forthcoming).
12. *New York Times,* May 19, 2008.
13. See Herbert McCabe, *Faith Within Reason* (London: Continuum, 2007), 108.
14. See Alain Badiou, *Saint Paul: The Foundation of Universalism* (Stanford: Stanford University Press, 2003), 55–56.
15. See Daniel Schwartz, *Aquinas on Friendship* (Oxford: Clarendon, 2007), 6.
16. See Terry Eagleton, *After Theory* (London: Allen Lane/Penguin, 2003), Ch. 6.
17. This presents me with an occasion for recounting an execrable Marxist joke of my own invention. The directors of an oil company were concerned that one of its plants was losing money hand over fist, managed as it was by Evangelicals who based their commercial decisions on instructions from the voice of God. The directors accordingly sent in a troubleshooter, a tough-minded ex-military type. But his efforts were to no avail, and his superiors eventually had to extract the rational colonel from the mystical Shell.
18. Karl Marx, "Contribution to the Critique of Hegel's Philosophy of Right," in *Karl Marx: Early Writings,* ed. T. B. Bottomore (London: C.A. Watts, 1963), 44.
19. Quoted by Dan Hind, *The Threat to Reason* (London: Verso, 2007), 22.
20. Gilbert Achtar, "Religion and Politics Today," *Socialist Register* (London, 2008), 59.

CHAPTER TWO

## The Revolution Betrayed

1. Terry Eagleton, "Lunging, Flailing, Mispunching," *London Review of Books* (19 October 2006), 32.
2. Denys Turner, *Faith, Reason and the Existence of God* (Cambridge: Cambridge University Press), 230.
3. Stephen Mulhall, *Philosophical Myths of the Fall* (Princeton, N.J.: Princeton University Press, 2005), 22.
4. Daniel C. Dennett, *Breaking the Spell: Religion as a Natural Phenomenon* (London: Penguin, 2007), 9.
5. See, for example, Kermode's *The Sense of an Ending* (Oxford: Oxford University Press, 1967) and *The Genesis of Secrecy* (Cambridge, Mass.: Harvard University Press, 1979), both of which display a subtle grasp of theological issues on the part of a resolutely secular critic.
6. Karl Barth, *Church Dogmatics,* vol. 4, Part 1 (Edinburgh: T. and T. Clark, 1961), 531.
7. Herbert McCabe, *Faith Within Reason* (London: Continuum, 2007), 46.
8. Melvin Hill, ed., *Hannah Arendt: The Recovery of the Public World* (New York: St. Martin's, 1979), 334–35.
9. See Dan Hind, *The Threat to Reason* (London: Verso, 2007), passim.
10. Charles Taylor, *A Secular Age* (Cambridge, Mass.: Belknap Press of Harvard University Press), 332.
11. See John Milbank and Catherine Pickstock, *Truth in Aquinas* (London: Routledge, 2001), and Fergus Kerr, *After Aquinas* (Oxford: Blackwell, 2002).
12. A point made by John E Smith, "Faith, Belief and the Problem of Rationality," in *Rationality and Religious Belief,* ed. C. F. Delaney (Notre Dame, Ind.: Notre Dame Press, 1979).
13. Richard Dawkins, *The God Delusion* (Boston: Houghton Mifflin, 2008), 271.

14. Alastair Crooke, "The Naïve Armchair Warriors Are Fighting A Delusional War," *Guardian* (24 March 2008).
15. I have written at greater length on this subject in *Holy Terror* (Oxford: Oxford University Press, 2005), Ch. 1.
16. See Walter Benjamin, "Theses on the Philosophy of History," in *Illuminations*, ed. Hannah Arendt (London: Collins/Fontana, 1973).
17. Ibid., 256.
18. Quoted by Detlev Claussen, *Theodor W. Adorno: One Last Genius* (Cambridge, Mass.: Harvard University Press, 2008), 338.
19. See Max Horkheimer and Theodor Adorno, *Dialectic of Enlightenment* (New York: Herder and Herder, 1972).
20. Quoted in Rush Rhees, *Ludwig Wittgenstein: Personal Recollections* (Oxford: Basil Blackwell, 1981), 101.
21. The landowner in question was apparently an ancestor of Aisling Foster, wife of the Irish historian Roy Foster, whose work I have occasionally seen fit to criticize from a radical viewpoint. *Plus ça change* . . .
22. See Pankaj Mishra, "The Burmese Monks' Spiritual Strength Proves Religion Has a Role in Politics," *Guardian* (1 October 2007).
23. Aijaz Ahmad, "Islam, Islamisms and the West," *Socialist Register* (London: Merlin, 2008), 12.
24. Ibid., 14.
25. Ibid., 29.
26. Ibid., 25.
27. Ibid., 26.
28. Ibid., 37.

## CHAPTER THREE
## Faith and Reason

1. See Robert Pape, *Dying to Win: The Strategic Logic of Suicide Terrorism* (New York: Random House, 2005).

2. Slavoj Žižek, *In Defence of Lost Causes* (London: Verso, 2008), 31.
3. Herbert McCabe, *Faith Within Reason* (London: Continuum, 2007), 13.
4. See Alain Badiou, *Being and Event* (London: Continuum, 2005).
5. See Terry Eagleton, *Trouble with Strangers* (Oxford: Wylie-Blackwell, 2008), Part 3, Ch.9.
6. See Jean-Yves Lacoste, "Perception, Transcendence and the Experience of God," in *Transcendence and Phenomenology,* ed. Peter M. Candler Jr. and Conor Cunningham (London: SCM Press, 2007), 15.
7. Christopher Hitchens, *God Is Not Great* (London: Atlantic, 2007), 5. Further references to this work will be provided in parentheses after quotations.
8. Dan Hind, *The Threat to Reason* (London: Verso, 2007), 64.
9. Denys Turner, *Faith, Reason and the Existence of God* (Cambridge: Cambridge University Press), 232.
10. Ludwig Wittgenstein, *On Certainty,* quoted in Anthony Kenny, ed., *The Wittgenstein Reader* (Oxford: Blackwell, 1994), 254.
11. Charles Taylor, *A Secular Age* (Cambridge, Mass.: Belknap Press of Harvard University Press, 2007), 835. The quotation from Dawkins is given by Taylor without reference.
12. See Charles Taylor, *Sources of the Self* (Cambridge: Cambridge University Press, 1989), Part II.
13. See Terry Eagleton, *Sweet Violence: The Idea of the Tragic* (Oxford: Blackwell, 2003), 258–59.

## CHAPTER FOUR
## Culture and Barbarism

1. Quoted by Dan Hind, *The Threat to Reason* (London: Verso, 2007), 70.
2. Catherine Gallagher, "The Rise of Fictionality," in *The Novel,*

*Volume 1: History, Geography, and Culture,* ed. Franco Moretti (Princeton, N.J.: Princeton University Press, 2006), 336–63.

3. Ibid., 346.
4. John Milbank, "Only Theology Saves Metaphysics: On the Modalities of Terror," in *Belief and Metaphysics,* ed. Peter M. Candler Jr. and Conor Cunningham (London: SCM Press, 2007), 455.
5. Aijaz Ahmad, "Islam, Islamisms and the West," *Socialist Register* (London: Merlin, 2008), 21.
6. See, for example, Richard Rorty, *Contingency, Irony, and Solidarity* (Cambridge: Cambridge University Press, 1989), and Stanley Fish, *Doing What Comes Naturally* (Oxford: Oxford University Press, 1989).
7. Asef Bayat, "Islamism and Empire: The Incongruous Nature of Islamist Anti-Imperialism," *Socialist Register* (London: Merlin, 2008), 43 and 49.
8. See Terry Eagleton, *The Illusions of Postmodernism* (Oxford: Basil Blackwell, 1996), Ch. 1.
9. For a powerful statement of this view, see Raymond Williams, *Modern Tragedy* (London: Chatto and Windus, 1966), Part 1, Ch. 4.

# Index